PUBLIC OWNERSHIP
AND ACCOUNTABILITY

PUBLIC OWNERSHIP
AND ACCOUNTABILITY

The Canadian Experience

Lloyd D. Musolf

HARVARD UNIVERSITY PRESS

Cambridge, Massachusetts

1 9 5 9

Distributed in Great Britain by
Oxford University Press
London

With this book the author pays tribute to Vassar College
on the occasion of its centennial.

Library of Congress Catalog Card Number 59–10319

Printed in the United States of America

TO THE MEMORY OF MY MOTHER

Preface

A common feature of our twentieth-century world is the accomplishment of certain public functions of an economic or social character through what are generally called "public corporations," institutions operated under government auspices but with varying degrees of freedom from government. Although most of these bodies are little known to the public, a few are, and some of these may even be recognized easily through their initials, such as the T.V.A. in the United States, the B.B.C. in Great Britain, and the C.B.C. in Canada. Public corporations are found in a great variety of countries — in new nations seeking to modernize their economies as well as in mature states striving for more flexibility in their administration of public policies, in dictatorships as well as democracies, in nations under capitalism as well as those under democratic socialism. In short, it is apparent that they are not creatures of a single climate of opinion, and even the conditions under which they are employed may vary considerably.

The attributes which make them appealing to a puzzling array of governments are their capabilities for directness of action, flexibility, and freedom from some of the red tape that encumbers ordinary governmental activities. In its broadest form this freedom might enable a corporation to retain its earnings and employ them as it wishes rather than being forced to depend on annual legislative appropriations and explicit spending directions; to acquire and sell property, make contracts, and perform other actions of a legal person; and to hire and fire employees without regard to ordinary civil service restrictions. In Western democracies, at least, a government agency may sometimes be called a public corporation without possessing all of these powers. This is so for at least two reasons. The popularity of the corporate device has sometimes produced an indiscriminate resort to it, with the result that, in a given country, public corporations may have little but the name in common. In addition, for corporations to possess the full range of powers has frequently been viewed by governments as a threat to their own operating responsibility.

To summarize the current situation, public corporations are often deemed to be useful instruments of modern government provided that they can be fitted into the governmental framework. "The great increase in the number of state-owned-and-operated business enterprises during the last decade," Harold Seidman, a perceptive student of government corporations, wrote in 1954, "has confronted almost every nation with a basic dilemma: how can the operating and financial flexibility required for the successful conduct of a business enterprise be reconciled with the need for controls to assure public accountability and consistency in public policy?"

Several points may be noted briefly here about the problem as it pertains to democracies. All governments share an apprehension about permitting an agency to act independently, and dictatorships, least of all, can allow complete autonomy to public corporations. The additional dilemma faced by democracies is that their governments are answerable to the electorate, and no part of the government can be permitted to weaken this arrangement. The thread of accountability can not be broken off at the point where public corporations are located. At the same time, the controls placed over corporations ought not stifle initiative and curb flexibility. To

arrive at a working balance between freedom and account-/
ability is an exercise in artful government.

Given the importance of the problem of accountability,
studies of the manner in which specific governments are dealing with it should prove of value. The experience of the Canadian government, it is submitted, is particularly worthy of
note. Canada has made a serious and sophisticated attempt to
deal with the problem. Although several excellent articles
and chapters in books have touched on the Canadian experience, it has never received more extended treatment. Finally,
because of Canada's position in the world, its experience may
be at least partly applicable to other countries. Canada
stands somewhere in the middle when nations are arrayed
in terms of size and importance. Her economy has characteristics found in both mature and underdeveloped countries.
Her form of government resembles that of many other nations. For some Americans this book might be of interest primarily because of the country dealt with rather than because
of the topic of corporate accountability. Canada's strategic
importance to North American defense, her role in NATO
and the UN, the protests of her political leaders about American trade policy, the growth of American investments in
Canada, increasing American dependence on Canadian raw
materials, the building of the St. Lawrence Seaway — these
and other factors have sharpened Americans' awareness of
their northern neighbors. Knowledge of Canadian institutions and processes of government, never great in the United
States, has most assuredly not kept pace with this awakening
interest. (It must be said, however, that the subject matter of
the present volume appears to be rather unfamiliar to many
Canadians as well.) This particular American was first moved
to investigate the accountability of Canadian public corporations through his speculations about the role of public ownership in a country similar to the United States in economic and

social background and to Great Britain in governmental institutions and certain cultural traditions. The differing experiences of America and Britain with public ownership and accountability prompted a curiosity about the handling of the problem in a nation responsive to both British and American stimuli but quite capable of charting an independent course.

It is appropriate at this point to state what this study does not cover. There has been no attempt in these pages to deal with such other important problems of public corporations as financing, internal management, personnel administration, and legal status, though passing references may be made to some of these topics. Nor will there be found here adequate descriptions of the operations of individual corporations. To deal with either of these sets of topics properly, separate studies would be required; to attempt to deal with them in this volume might only tend to blur its purpose.

In approaching the topic of corporate accountability in Canada, several basic assumptions were made. Although they are scarcely novel, they deserve mention here by way of clarifying the author's purpose. First, it was assumed that controls over corporations could only be discussed in a larger context: the climate of opinion that surrounds public corporations in Canada. This context the first chapter attempts to provide, largely by picturing the role of the more entrepreneurial public corporations, as a rule the best-known and most controversial group in any country. Secondly, it was assumed that the essence of the Canadian story could be found in a host of individual developments. Frequent recourse to specific examples seemed to be justified by the Canadian reputation for concern with specifics rather than with theories. Finally, a reasonable caution dictated that the choice of examples be confined to the national government, for provincial developments — while definitely worthy of scrutiny

— are too varied for inclusion. Even at the national level, the existence of forty public corporations means that complete coverage must often be sacrificed. If, however, portions of the study seem to overstress the importance of a handful of the better-known corporations, this bias largely reflects the record of corporate development in Canada. Chronologically, few examples will be found to date beyond the Liberal era that came to an end with the elections of June 1957 and April 1958. Such changes as were accomplished by the Diefenbaker government through August 1958 have been noted at appropriate points in the manuscript, although their full significance can not yet be assessed.

Because of the nature of the investigation and the scarcity of secondary materials, the author has relied heavily on governmental documents, personal interviews, and written communications. He wishes, therefore, to record his deep appreciation for the valuable assistance and wholehearted cooperation given him by many persons in Ottawa. Although the list of those who gave very kindly of their knowledge, wisdom, and time is much too long to enumerate, the completion of the book owes most to the following persons. Mr. H. R. Balls, formerly director, Financial Administration and Accounting Policy Division, Department of Finance, and now comptroller of the Treasury, was unfailingly generous and helpful over a period of several years in furnishing advice and information and in criticizing the chapters in draft form. Miss Mabel James, librarian, Department of Finance, provided working space in the departmental library, aided in discovering sources, and checked footnote references for several chapters. Mr. Elmer Driedger, assistant deputy minister and parliamentary counsel, Department of Justice, dispensed valuable advice about statutory provisions that refer to public corporations. Of the numerous corporate officials who were interviewed, special mention should be made of the help given by the Messrs. L. C. Audette, W. D. Low, and Bernard Drabble. Professors R. O. MacFarlane and D. C. Rowat of the School of Public Administration, Carleton University, advanced the author's education in Canadian government through numerous conversations and by permitting him to visit certain graduate seminars. Miss Hilda Gifford, librarian, Carleton University, gave much initial help on bibliography. Professors J. A. Corry and J. E. Hodgetts of Queens University and Mr. F. C. Milligan of the Department of Defence Production provided encouragement and advice at some stages of the research. Emeritus Professor Arthur W. Mac-Mahon of Columbia University read the concluding chapter in draft and made useful suggestions. The author is indebted to Mrs. Ruth Ashman, secretary, Department of Political Science, Vassar College, for great patience and skill in typing the manuscript. Finally, he wishes to record his appreciation for the forbearance of his wife and his academic colleagues.

Financially the completion of the study owes much to Vassar College. A faculty fellowship permitted residence in Ottawa during the academic year of 1954–55. A travel grant from the Lucy Maynard Salmon Fund permitted visits to Ottawa during the summer of 1957. A debt of gratitude is also owed to the Earhart Foundation of Ann Arbor, Michigan, which furnished travel funds for the summer of 1956.

A version of Chapter 1 appeared in *The American Political Science Review* for June 1956, and the author is grateful to the executive director of the American Political Science Association for permission to use an adaptation of the article. For the shortcomings of this study, the author, needless to say, deserves sole blame.

L. D. M.

Vassar College
December 1958

Contents

Tables

PUBLIC OWNERSHIP
AND ACCOUNTABILITY

1

Pragmatism and Public Enterprise

In any country whose economy rests mainly on private enterprise, government activities that are in some degree entrepreneurial might be expected to be somewhat anomalous. Yet, the way in which such activities are *actually* regarded is a function of many variables, including the self-sufficiency of the private sector of the economy, the prominence of ideological considerations, and the nation's own peculiar sense of destiny. This chapter attempts to picture the role of public enterprise in Canada. In this particular "free enterprise" garden, how should the public enterprise plant be described — as a creeper vine, a hothouse flower, or a hardy but unspectacular perennial? How has it affected its surroundings and, in turn, been affected by them? As a beginning, a brief sketch of the principal features, together with some reference to the American situation, may help to establish the setting.

On the surface, Canadian public enterprise resembles its American counterpart in several ways. In each country the government has acted in response to the needs of the moment rather than on the basis of long-range plans or considerations of organizational symmetry. Too, markedly different purposes have been served by public enterprise in both Canada and the United States. A Canadian compilation made in 1954 listed five credit and financial agencies, eight commodity trading and procurement agencies, a dozen producing and business agencies, and sixteen management and research agencies.[1] Within each of these categories a similar diversity exists. The first category, for example, contains agencies whose respective functions are to lend to farmers, insure exporters against nonpayment by foreign buyers, carry out a variety of activities in the field of housing, make loans to small industry, and perform all the functions of a central bank.

Equally familiar to Americans and Canadians is the virtually automatic use of the corporate form for public enterprise. As in the United States, this organizational form has benefited from the respect in which it is held (for different reasons) by both businessmen and reformers. This phenomenon, in turn, has been perpetuated by the absence of a systematic attempt in either country to nationalize industry, using the corporate form as the vehicle. As a final point of similarity, haphazard employment of the public corporation for a number of purposes, variety in organizational attributes of different corporations, and concern about maintaining democratic control over corporations have combined to produce remedial legislation in each country. The Canadian counterpart of the Government Corporation Control Act of 1945 is the Financial Administration Act of 1951.[2] Although a half-dozen corporations are not covered by the act,[3] the remaining "Crown corporations" are classified into one of three categories on the basis of general purpose and degree of financial independence. This classification is as follows: *departmental corporations* — Agricultural Stabilization Board, Atomic Energy Control Board, Canadian Maritime Commission, Director of Soldier Settlement, The Director, the Veterans Land Act, Dominion Coal Board, Fisheries Prices Support Board, National Gallery of Canada, National Research Council, Unemployment Insurance Commission; *agency corporations* — Atomic Energy of Canada Limited, Canadian Arsenals Limited, Canadian Commercial Corporation, Canadian Patents and Development Limited, Crown Assets Disposal Corporation, Defence Construction (1951) Limited, Federal District Commission, National Battlefields Commission, National Harbors Board, Northern Canada Power Commission, Park Steamship Company Limited; *proprietary corporations* — Canadian Broadcasting Corporation, Canadian Farm Loan Board, Canadian National Railways, Canadian National (West Indies) Steamships Limited, Canadian Overseas Telecommunication Corporation, Central Mortgage and Housing Corporation, Eldorado Aviation Limited, Eldorado Mining and Refining Limited, Export Credits Insurance Corporation, Northern Transportation Company Limited, Polymer Corporation Limited, St. Lawrence Seaway Authority, Trans-Canada Air Lines; *corporations not classified by the act* — Bank of Canada, Canadian Wheat Board, Eastern Rockies Forest Conservation Board, Halifax Relief Commission, Industrial Development Bank, Northern Ontario Pipe Line Crown Corporation.[4] "Departmental" corporations, at present ten in number, are described by the statute as "responsible for administrative, supervisory or regulatory services of a governmental nature." In terms of financial treatment, the act lumps them with departments, and the only apparent reason for retaining the corporate form is to simplify processes of litigation.[5] The financial treatment accorded "agency" and "proprietary" corporations — the other groupings established by the statute — is similar to that ordinarily associated with corporations. By the terms of the act, agency corporations are given somewhat less fiscal freedom than proprietary corporations,[6] but one observer has noted that "there is apparently no single factor determining into which category a corporation will be placed."[7] In differentiating the two groups according to purpose, the act describes agency corporations (now eleven in number) as engaged in trading, service, procurement, construction, or disposal activities, and proprietary corporations (now thirteen in number) as engaged in lending, financial, commercial, or industrial operations. Unlike agency corporations, proprietary corporations are "ordinarily required" to conduct their operations without appropriations, but in practice this description does not fit all of them.

In all likelihood, the most obvious difference [8] between public enterprise at the national level in the two countries is the far greater scope of Canadian operations in the fields of transportation, communication, and (to some extent) production. Public corporations operate one of Canada's two large railroad systems (with such subsidiary services as express, telegraph, and hotels) and the only transcontinental systems in civil aviation, radio, and television. They conduct commercial operations at seven important harbors, mine and refine uranium, produce atomic energy and synthetic rubber, operate shipping lines, and furnish transportation and electric power facilities in areas of northern Canada.

The significant fact about the substantial scope of Canadian public enterprise in certain important economic areas, however, is that it does not justify automatic inferences about a pro-government ownership sentiment any more than Canada's reputation for financial conservatism justifies automatic inferences about its choice of private enterprise for each and every task. This will be more apparent after a review of the factors which delimit public enterprise territory in Canada.

THE BOUNDARIES OF PUBLIC ENTERPRISE

The operational area for government enterprise is bounded at its extremes by two familiar Canadian landmarks: (1) the tradition that the national government should act aggressively to establish and maintain national economic unity; and (2) the tradition of an economic system anchored on private enterprise. The first factor argues for the creation of sufficient government enterprise to assure accomplishment of the national goals; the second signifies the absence of an ideological drive to place industry in the government's hands.

The vital part played by the state in developing Canada has been noted often by the country's economists. "The role of the state in the economic life of Canada," Professor Alexander Brady has remarked, "is really the modern history of Canada." [9] Confederation itself, another economist has argued, "can be interpreted as a political adaptation to the unfavourable impact of the first industrial revolution on Canada." [10] At the very least, the Confederation document — the British North America Act — obligated the national government to undertake a commercial venture in order to bind the Maritime Provinces to Quebec and Ontario. Soon after satisfying this obligation by building the Intercolonial Railway, the government heavily subsidized the Canadian Pacific in order to reinforce British Columbia's links to the nation and to provide the first transcontinental railroad. The government also built canals, provided protective tariffs and bonuses for secondary industry, and opened the western lands to settlement. These actions performed the vital function of supplementing the inadequate efforts of private capital. Generally speaking, they were popular, as Sir John A. MacDonald's "National Policy" in particular demonstrated.[11]

The stimuli which made the state take an active role — "the pioneer nature of the country, the physical structure of the half-continent, the imperial sweep of settlement after 1867, the influence of the interacting ideas and institutions of Britain and the United States, and the quick response of the whole society to the advance of western industrialism" [12] — retain much of their force today. Partly this is so because it has been characteristic of Western society, in whose dynamic nature Canada shares, to advance constantly its concepts of minimum requirements. Thus, an old field of concern for the state — transportation and communication — has continued to challenge the government as new inventions have come along. In the case of transcontinental aviation and radio broadcasting, for example, the government chose to create public corporations in the 1930's to operate these services rather than to allow chaotic private development. As examples of relatively recent actions designed to bind the nation together, the reasoning involved is worth considering briefly.

The swift advance in the commercial possibilities of air travel — as demonstrated by private air lines in the United States — had caught Canada by surprise. Private enterprise, in the opinion of the Liberal government, was not up to the task of providing the nation with efficient transcontinental air service. Lamenting the fact that a "score or more" of private companies had ended on the financial junkheap, C. D. Howe, minister of transport, told the House of Commons in 1937: "Our task in Canada is to set up this service without all the lost motion that has been expended during the past ten years." [13] The creation of Trans-Canada Air Lines, a corporate subsidiary of Canadian National Railways, followed. At a later date, in reviewing the airline's remarkable progress, Howe tied T.C.A. into the tradition of national development in the following words: "Facilities for transportation and communication have been among our most powerful tools in the fashioning of Canadian unity . . . T.C.A. serves in the same high tradition . . . Canadian distances have already lost much of their old significance . . . and a new sense of nationhood is being fostered by Canada's new accessibility to its citizens. In particular, Canadian industry and business have received a major stimulus from air transport." [14]

The creation of the Canadian Radio Broadcasting Commission (predecessor of the Canadian Broadcasting Corporation) in 1932 demonstrated that government ownership for the sake of national development was not a monopoly of the Liberal party. Radio broadcasting had to be under government auspices for three reasons, Conservative Prime Minister R. B. Bennett told the House:

First of all, this country must be assured of complete Canadian control of broadcasting from Canadian sources, free from foreign interference or influence . . . [so that] national consciousness may be fostered and sustained and national unity still further strengthened. . . .

Secondly, no other scheme . . . can ensure . . . equal enjoyment of the benefits and pleasures of radio broadcasting. . . .

[Thirdly] . . . the air itself . . . is a natural resource over which we have complete jurisdiction . . . I believe that there is no government in Canada that does not regret today that it has parted with some of these natural resources for considerations wholly inadequate and on terms that do not reflect the principle under which the crown holds the natural resources in trust for all the people.[15]

The years since the onset of World War II have witnessed a merger of the national development theme with that of national defense. Each reinforces the strength of the other. Does it aid defense or development more when, for example, public corporations mine and refine uranium or build transportation and electric power systems in remote, primitive areas of the country? The pace of events still outruns the capabilities of private interests in conquering Canadian geography alone, even if business wished to devote its efforts to relatively unprofitable projects. In view of world events and Canada's own ambitions, it is evident that continued government action of this sort will be needed in the foreseeable future.

The second familiar Canadian landmark that affects the scope of public enterprise is the prime role of private enterprise in the economy. The logic which gave an active economic role to the state has never been extended (except in platforms of the Cooperative Commonwealth Federation, the democratic socialist party) to the nationalization of industry. No huge existing industries have been taken over by the government, unless one includes the acquisition of the bankrupt railroads during World War I.[16]

In the instance of the railroads, not only was the prosperous Canadian Pacific left intact, but the reasoning by which the other private railroads were acquired demonstrates the limited role of sentiment favoring public ownership. The onset of war had abruptly shut off the flow of immigration and of foreign capital, a situation which immediately threatened the solvency of several railroads that had just reached a period in their development when earnings might offset the heavy initial expenditure of capital and begin to repay extensive government loans made in the developmental period. The *Debates* of the House of Commons reflect the shock of the members at the grim turn of events — a shock made all the greater because of the rosy vision of Canada's future entertained especially by members from the prairie provinces. Although much time and energy were spent in recriminations and attempts to fix the blame for the "needless duplication" and "costly overbuilding" of railroads, the problem of what to do remained. Public ownership was arrived at only after a painful canvass of various alternatives. To let the railroads go into receivership was not considered a viable alternative because foreign investors had relied on the guarantees given by the national and provincial governments in connection with bonds issued by the railroads.[17] Default on the guarantees, it was felt, would affect Canada's credit adversely at the very time it was fighting a great war. Further loans to the railroads were out of the question because it was suspected that public opinion would not tolerate them, a feeling summed up by the Conservative Minister of Finance when he declared: "If the public does the financing, the public should enjoy the ultimate reward." [18] Government leaders were certain that public opinion would not allow the bankrupt roads to fall into the hands of the gigantic and prosperous Canadian Pacific.[19] Finally, once a segment of a transcontinental road was acquired from a bankrupt company, it was financially necessary to take over the rest of the line.[20] Thus, the acquisition of the Canadian Northern was followed by that of the Grand Trunk and the Grand Trunk Pacific.

In emphasizing that the Canadian government more or less "backed into" ownership of the railroads, it is not intended to imply that public ownership sentiment was nonexistent. As a matter of fact, the *Debates* contain considerable evidence that the House was well aware of popular sentiment, especially in Ontario and the West, favoring government ownership.[21] Nevertheless, it is apparent that this sentiment did not govern the situation. The Borden government drew a sharp line between taking over bankrupt railroads and wholesale nationalization, rejecting the latter as highly detrimental "to the credit of the Dominion and to our prospects for future financing." [22]

Just as pragmatic considerations outweighed public ownership sentiment in the acquisition of the bankrupt railroads, so they have prevailed in subsequent ventures in public enterprise. In fact, freed of the elements of surprise and reluctance manifest in the railroad situation, the government has appeared to weigh practical aspects even more deliberately. One of the best illustrations is found in a debate on the government's proposals for liberalization of credit to small businessmen, farmers, and fishermen in 1944. The flexibility of the Liberal government's approach was demonstrated by the fact that an Industrial Development Bank was proposed to handle loans to small businessmen, while the commercial banks were to be agents in making government-backed loans to farmers and fishermen. Highly practical reasons were offered for employing public enterprise in one instance and rejecting its use in the other.[23] In the course of debate government spokesmen were called upon to defend their stand against nationalization of all commercial banks, which had been demanded by the Co-operative Commonwealth Federation. The Minister of Finance took the position that: "The question of nationalization of an industry or a specific firm should not be one of ideology. We should neither shrink from nationalization because of an economic philosophy based on fear, nor embrace it rashly . . . We should use it only where it alone can serve the public interest or can serve it better than any alternative form of organization. Commercial banking, I am convinced, is not one of those cases." [24] In his rebuttal, M. J. Coldwell, the C.C.F. leader, recited a number of alleged inadequacies in the banking system and emphasized that "It is on these grounds then, that we call for the national ownership and control of the financial system, and particularly the banks; not, as the minister suggested, on some doctrinaire theory that their socialization will destroy the present system." [25] This denial of a doctrinaire approach, it may be noted, came from a source usually identified as one of the most doctrinaire on the subject of public enterprise.

A highly pragmatic attitude, then, has consistently demonstrated its usefulness in any situation where the traditions of national economic development and private enterprise may come into conflict. This attitude has probably been able to emerge more easily because business and government are constrained by the circumstances toward moderation. Business cannot easily boast of an exclusive role in building the economy, as it tends to in the United States, for it is faced not merely with a history of government enterprise dating back to Confederation, but with an even more vital present. Furthermore, under the brand of Keynesianism practiced by the Canadian government, it has a close working arrangement with the government in the promotion of prosperity and industrial development.[26] Probably it is also restrained by a consciousness of its own limited strength, its vulnerability to a charge that subsidiaries of American corporations are prominent in its midst, and, less importantly, a fear that a reactionary stand might strengthen the hand of the C.C.F. and bring on nationalization. The government, for its part, has not exhibited — under either the Conservatives or the Liberals — any inclination to push public enterprise for its own sake; in this it has but mirrored its recognition and approval of private enterprise as the foundation of the economy. Although it has not shrunk from taking action necessary to attain the goal of economic unity, even if this has meant launching a commercial venture, it has done so only in response to demonstrated need.

This section has attempted to sketch a rough profile of Canadian public enterprise. The portrait takes fuller shape through consideration of some of the conditions under which public enterprise operates.

OPERATING CONDITIONS

The existence of public enterprise in a predominantly private enterprise economy inevitably poses certain problems of adjustment. Are units of public enterprise to be operated as a monopoly or in competition with business? Broadly speaking, shall public enterprise furnish an operating standard for private enterprise? Should the operating conditions of public enterprise be made as nearly like those of business as possible? An examination of the Canadian answers to these questions should help to evaluate the extent to which that country's public enterprise has affected, and in turn been affected by, a "free enterprise" setting.

It is consistent with the empirical nature of Canadian economic development that monopoly and competition exist side by side on the public enterprise scene without causing any apparent uneasiness. Public corporations have a monopoly in the production of synthetic rubber, atomic energy, and certain lines of munitions. Public enterprise is in direct competition with business in railroads, telegraph, and express services. It coexists with private enterprise but does not enter into direct competition with it in credit, radio and television broadcasting, and aviation — although changes are occurring in the last two fields. The line of reasoning which backs up the existence of each of these arrangements is worth examining briefly.

The justification for monopoly has ranged from the supposed inability of private enterprise to cope with a vital economic function to a desire to eliminate waste and duplication. The Crown companies created during World War II under the auspices of the Department of Munitions and Supply [27] are the foremost examples of the first line of reasoning. The criterion used by the Minister was as follows: "If private business was able to carry out the war objective, private business was given that opportunity. The government has created Crown companies only to undertake work that private industry was not willing to undertake." [28] For those few Crown companies not liquidated by the coming of peace, further justification had to be sought. By way of example, it was found for Polymer Corporation Limited, the country's sole manufacturer of synthetic rubber, in the argument that business was benefited at a time of uncertain supply of foreign rubber, that no private rubber industry existed in Canada, and that "We would be glad to sell the Polymer Corporation to private industry, if private industry would buy it." [29] As with Canadian Arsenals Limited, the needs of national defense also played an important part in perpetuating the government monopoly.[30]

Elimination of waste and duplication as an argument for monopoly is best illustrated by the field of civil aviation, where the government's airline has been the only transcontinental operator. The lesson derived from railroad overbuilding and resultant bankruptcy at the time of World War I was not lost on the Liberal government in creating Trans-Canada Air Lines in 1937. It was set up, the Minister of Transport said later, "to avoid the duplication of services that were the outgrowth of competitive building for profit in the field of surface transportation." [31] Its exclusive franchise recognized "the principle that our small population would not warrant competition on this route." [32]

Competition between public and private enterprise — as exemplified by the railroad industry — finds its justification in the incentives it furnishes.[33] In 1917, when public ownership of all Canadian railroads was being urged on him, the Conservative Minister of Railways and Canals voiced his doubt whether "a government monopoly would be a very great improvement upon a private monopoly" because "once the incentive to service, which is brought about by competition, is removed it is not so sure that a monopoly, even if it be a public monopoly, would be the best thing for the public." [34] One of the reasons given by Acting Prime Minister Sir Thomas White in 1919 for preserving the identity of the privately owned Canadian Pacific when other

railroads were being combined under government management was that "there should be two railway systems in this
country, one of which will be, so to speak, a check, in the
sense of efficiency in the administration, upon the other." [35]
The political virtues of this arrangement were recognized
by R. B. Bennett, the Conservative Prime Minister from 1930
to 1935, when he gave a prominent place in his successful
campaign of 1930 to the slogan, "Amalgamation? Never.
Competition? Ever." [36] But the depth of the feeling which
it evokes is perhaps best illustrated by the following statement of a leading Canadian economist: "It is the hope of
democracy in Canada that both [railroads] will continue to
strive earnestly but that neither will succeed, and that the
impossibility of running two competitive railways will continue ... We may hope that the aggressiveness of the Canadian Pacific Railway will keep politics out of the Canadian
National and that the aggressiveness of the Canadian National Railways will keep the Canadian Pacific out of politics and out of the Canadian Treasury, and that the results
will permit the continuation of democratic government." [37]

Despite the strength of the belief in railroad competition,
it would be misleading to assert that competition has seriously vied with monopoly as a guiding principle for public
enterprise in Canada. Granted the existence of the powerful
Canadian Pacific and the absence of an ideological drive
for nationalization of all railroads, nothing was left to a government which had inherited various bankrupt railroads but
to compete — and to compete vigorously — if the jumble of
roads was to survive. The announced determination to operate the system "as though it were a private corporation" [38]
and the appointment of a daring and experienced railroad
man to head it testified to the vigor of the attempt, at least.
Transcontinental aviation and radio, however, have offered
a contrast. Here private enterprise — partly because it

lacked the substantial subsidies furnished the Canadian Pacific — never succeeded in establishing transcontinental links, and, after public enterprise entered the field, was deliberately precluded from doing so by the Liberal government. Competition, in short, was highly touted only where no practicable alternative to competition was thought to exist. Outside the area encompassed by the railroads and their subsidiary services, a deliberate policy of noncompetition with business was in force, according to Liberal government leaders.[39] This policy reflected, and probably still reflects, political wisdom in Canada because it maintains freedom of action for those occasions when an extension of public enterprise is called for,[40] and at the same time undercuts the argument that nationalization is the inevitable consequence of such an extension.[41] Although the Conservatives have always endorsed the notion that government corporations should not, except in railroads, set out to compete with private operators, a more crucial question that faced the party when it came to power in 1957 was whether certain government corporations should be made to yield up their monopolies.

Well before the Conservative ascent to power, signs of unrest had gradually been accumulating in the areas of the public economy that lie on the border between monopoly and competition. In radio, television, and aviation — which have been split between public and private enterprise, with the major portion reserved to the government — circumstances favor continued, and perhaps increasing, friction. As the country becomes more heavily populated, industrialized, and wealthy, the "chosen instrument" policy, established in the pessimistic 1930's, runs the risk of appearing unsuited to a young and vigorous land. The Canadian Association of Radio and Television Broadcasters has long agitated for the right to form a network of private radio stations and thereby enter into direct competition with the Canadian Broadcasting Corporation.[42] This argument and its corollary — that the Corporation's regulatory powers over private radio stations should be turned over to an independent regulatory commission which would supervise the activities of both public and private radio — were steadfastly resisted by the Liberals, aided by the findings of a Royal Commission regarding the cultural needs of Canada.[43] The advent of television intensified this basic disagreement. Television's rapid progress in the United States under private auspices, the availability of American television to certain Canadian viewers while others did not have even the single C.B.C. channel available, the caution with which licenses for private television stations were granted by the C.B.C. — these factors brought government television, which has been plagued by the high cost of extending its services in a vast, bilingual country, under a certain amount of public disapproval. In response to growing agitation on these and other points, a Royal Commission on Broadcasting was appointed in December 1955. Its report, issued in March 1957, clearly endorsed the chosen instrument policy for network radio and television.[44] While conceding that the "forces of economics" are against a non-commercial broadcasting system, the Commission urged its continuance in order "to keep a Canadian identity and culture" (I, 287). Although the notion of an independent regulatory body was rejected (I, 130–136), a clearer internal separation of functions was advocated, along with the replacement of the present board with a Board of Broadcast Governors clearly responsible for all public and private broadcasting in Canada (I, 88–100). In acting on this report, the Diefenbaker government indicated early in its tenure that it intended to go beyond an internal separation of functions and that it would establish a separate regulatory body. This intention was carried out in a statute passed by the House of Commons in August 1958.[45] Although the effects of this legislation remain to be demonstrated, government leaders insisted in debate on the bill that the creation of an independent Board of Broadcast Governors to regulate broadcasting does not mean the end of the single national broadcasting system, but merely that the C.B.C. "will have to appear before the board if it wants a licence for a new station and be treated in the same way as any other person in that field." [46] Although this arrangement falls short of the private broadcasters' highest hopes, it represents a considerable advance, from their point of view, over the previous situation. The regulations promulgated by the new board will indicate the extent to which the relationship between public and private broadcasters has actually been altered. Part II of the statute re-established the C.B.C. as "a corporation . . . consisting of a President, a Vice-President and nine other directors" with the duty of "operating a national broadcasting service."

In aviation — where transcontinental routes have been monopolized by the government's airline, other domestic routes have been left to private industry, and international routes have been assigned to either — the situation has been more favorable for a switch to a policy of competition. There already exists a single powerful rival, Canadian Pacific Air Lines, offspring of the Canadian Pacific Railway and operator of all private international routes and nearly all of the private domestic routes. Trans-Canada Air Lines does not possess regulatory power over private interests, as did the Canadian Broadcasting Corporation, and only the timely intervention of the Liberal Cabinet prevented at least one significant inroad on the public monopoly in transcontinental aviation. In 1953, after the Air Transport Board had approved the application of Canadian Pacific

Air Lines to establish a competing air freight service across most of the continent, the Cabinet voided the action on the ground that the prospective volume of traffic did not yet justify duplicating the government's service.[47] The following year, the Cabinet made its first concession to competition in international routes when it approved a trans-Arctic service between Vancouver and Amsterdam, a shorter route to Europe than that used by Trans-Canada Air Lines. Under the present Conservative government, competition in domestic and transborder air service appears to be on the way to becoming a reality. Minister of Transport George M. Hees announced in February 1958 that "the gradual introduction of competition will be a good thing for the Canadian public and for Canadian aviation as a whole."[48] The cautious approach taken by the Conservatives toward the introduction of competition makes it plain that the departure from Liberal policy is not as drastic as it at first appears. The Minister was quite specific in stating that "While competition is desirable, it must be regulated, and should be introduced only where economic conditions indicate that more than one operator can carry on successfully without government subsidy." This statement is reminiscent of one made to Parliament five years earlier by C. D. Howe: "If sufficient travel develops to the point where competition is warranted, then certainly air routes may be entitled to competition."[49] The interparty differences seem to lie more in the timing of the introduction of competition than in the desirability of introducing it. Judging by the Minister's statement, the Conservatives do not intend to play favorites. Competition will be introduced on private routes, as well as those of T.C.A., and private air lines will be expected to serve nonsustaining areas, just as T.C.A. does. Rules such as these, if enforced, should demonstrate to private groups that competition with public corporations can entail stern responsibilities as well as glowing opportunities.

Reference to a current trend in the United States may bring the developments noted above into perspective. Under the so-called "businessman's administration" in the United States, the emphasis is frankly upon getting government *out of* competition with business. In fact, this was, to a degree, one of the terms of reference of the second Hoover Commission.[50] At those points where Canadian business coexists with public enterprise but is restricted in its actions (radio, television, aviation), the businessman's aim is to get *into* competition with the government. This seeming contrast yields quickly to a twofold explanation. First, it is apparent that the dissimilar aims listed above are but two different stages of a drive by business to improve its position vis-à-vis public enterprise. Second, the contrast is explainable in terms of each nation's economic development. In order to assure the nation of essential economic services it was not necessary for the American government to pre-empt certain vital areas of the economy, as the Canadian government was forced to do. Where Canadian business is confronted with pre-empted areas it naturally raises a clamor to enter the forbidden preserves. As economic growth continues, a logical expectation is that the forbidden grass will appear ever greener. A view such as the following, excerpted from an editorial in a Conservative newspaper, may be given more frequent expression in the future: ". . . no economic or political principle in this country says that public ownership should be without competition, that it should have a right to monopoly." [51]

The second question posed at the beginning of this section — whether Canadian public enterprise furnishes an operating standard for private enterprise — could be answered in the negative until recently. Undoubtedly, the

Canadian National Railways sets a standard for the Canadian Pacific in the sense that the latter is conscious of a need to remain efficient in order to be certain of not being absorbed by its rival. The C.N.R.'s power to set standards is greatly limited by circumstances, however. Originally it had to integrate the operations of various inherited railroads, whereas the C.P.R. has combined its natural advantage of a unified structure with a fine record of efficiency. Consequently, the Canadian Pacific, more often than not, has been the pacesetter. Doubt has also been expressed — in various quarters and for different reasons — whether even such relatively similar forms of enterprise as the C.N.R. and the C.P.R. can be truly compared.[52] Finally, direct competition as a method of setting standards for private enterprise was arrived at almost accidentally in the case of the railroads and was not copied. Once away from the example of the railroads, not even the milder "yardstick" form of competition, as exemplified by the T.V.A., has prevailed as a method of assuring that public enterprise sets a standard.[53] Now, however, the Conservative government is in a position to let public enterprise set a standard in aviation and, to a lesser extent, in radio and television. T.C.A.'s widely conceded record of excellence will furnish a real challenge to private airlines.

To the third question — whether the operating conditions of public enterprise should be made as nearly like those of business as possible — the Canadian answer appears to be more strongly in the affirmative than might be expected. Two very different lines of reasoning support this answer: first, a concern that public enterprise should obtain a measure of business's secrecy and unity of purpose in operation, and secondly, that public enterprise should be exposed to as many of the normal business costs as feasible.

Influential in popularizing the first line of reasoning was

the accident that the first major commercial venture of the Canadian government in this century involved strenuous competition with a private firm. From the start it was recognized by government leaders that the Canadian National Railways needed privacy and autonomy in its daily operations in order to compete with its able rival. Although the Liberals fought this notion vigorously as an invasion of parliamentary responsibility, they espoused it themselves after replacing the Union government (a wartime coalition of Conservatives plus Liberals who had left their party over the issue of conscription) in December 1921. Thus, Prime Minister Mackenzie King asserted that under the Liberals the president of the C.N.R. would always have "precisely the same degree of latitude and freedom as the shareholders of the Canadian Pacific would give to Mr. Beatty [the C.P.R. president]." [54] This point of view matched that of his Unionist predecessor who — exasperated at the flow of questions about the C.N.R. — asked the House: ". . . how is the Canadian National Railways directorate going to make a success . . . of its efforts to compete with the Canadian Pacific, if every day it is subject to having every action . . . disclosed to the public and to its competitor while . . . the competitor need disclose nothing at all?" [55] Business concepts, then, exerted a powerful influence at the formative stage in the development of the public corporation, even though it was always apparent that the public corporation could never attain the degree of autonomy characteristic of its opposite number.[56]

When public enterprise expands and diversifies in a "free enterprise" country, it is apt to run into a feeling that various costs confronting business should also be charged to the operations of public enterprises. Curiously enough, this belief — which operates as a second factor in rendering public enterprise more like private — seems to have produced more tangible results so far in Canada than in the United States, despite the extremely vigorous stand of American business groups on the matter. Several bits of evidence in support of this statement may be cited.

Since 1952 the government's "proprietary corporations" — the group most nearly comparable to private enterprise — have had to pay the federal income tax at the same rate as private corporations.[57] Levied in response to mounting agitation since World War II,[58] the tax was justified by the Minister of Finance as designed "to make the financial statements of these crown companies more comparable with private industry, and make it easier to assess the relative efficiency of their operations." [59] Moreover, the hope was expressed by another government spokesman that the provinces would now tax their own public corporations and thereby put them "in a position where a better or more accurate comparison can be made of the relative efficiency of publicly-owned corporations competing in the same field." [60]

Two other tax changes may be cited in support of the contention that the Canadian government has attempted to lessen the difference in operating costs between public and private enterprise. One is the government's instructions to public corporations to conclude agreements with municipalities for the payment of grants in lieu of taxes.[61] Undoubtedly, the principal reason for the directive was to satisfy the clamor of tax-hungry municipalities.[62] The connection between this step and the one just reviewed, however, was made plain by the Parliamentary Assistant to the Minister of Finance, who stated that "the principle is really the same in payment by federal corporations of both municipal taxes and federal taxes." [63] A second pertinent tax change, announced in the Budget Speech of 1952, effected a substantial reduction in the federal income tax paid by privately owned public utilities engaged in the generation and distribution of electrical energy, gas, or steam.[64] Although it was adopted chiefly to forestall applications for rate increases by these companies, the Minister of Finance agreed with a member of the opposition that "This clause will have a tendency to bring more nearly into line the activities of privately-owned utility corporations and those of publicly-owned corporations." [65]

CONCLUSION

Canadian public enterprise, as the foregoing pages demonstrate, is complex in character and not lacking in paradoxical elements. It occupies only a modest segment of the economy, but it literally links the nation together. Although it has had a long history, it has never won the emotional allegiance of Canadians. Without an ideological drive to sustain it, it has still achieved a vital place in the economy because of its decisive importance in the continuing task of nation-building. Exceedingly pragmatic as Canadian public enterprise appears to be, the consistency with which it is used in situations involving challenges to national economic unity virtually gives its motivating factor the status of a theory. Though specific examples of public enterprise may be relatively uncontroversial, the four (now three) parliamentary parties have not hesitated to express varying notions about public ownership generally, ranging from a reduction in its scope to nationalization of industry. In the face of this activity by party orators, however, "The average Canadian has something less than enthusiasm for arguing the merit of private versus public enterprise." [66]

Complex though its character may be, Canadian public enterprise generally obtains more candid and dispassionate treatment than is customary in the United States. Wholesale approval or condemnation of the principle of public ownership frequently yields to honest attempts to judge the performance of individual units of public enterprise.[67] Neither the extension of public enterprise nor, on the other hand, its taxation, appear to have aroused major displays of public emotion. When such contrasting developments can occur almost simultaneously and in a relatively calm atmosphere, the explanation must go deeper than the difference between Canadian and American temperaments or forms of government, significant as these matters may be. Judging from the picture which has been sketched in these pages, the principal explanation may be that in Canada *laissez faire* never had the opportunity — though force of circumstances — to reach the status of a dogma or of an emotional catchword. It became neither a folk myth to which eternal allegiance was due nor a *bête noire* to be overcome at all costs. Consequently, to a very real extent the guiding criterion in Canada is that expressed by C. D. Howe, who has been, fittingly, both a prolific launcher of public corporations and a highly successful businessman: "... there is only one test of the strength and weakness of either private operation or governmental operation, namely, which can best serve the need of the public of Canada." [68] The reservation which must accompany this statement — and which points up Canada's basic economic conservatism and kinship to the United States — is found in another quotation, this one by former Prime Minister Louis St. Laurent: "I think we are all most happy when free enterprise does what is required to be done and public authorities do not have to intervene." [69]

The status that public enterprise has attained in Canada has some meaning for the problem of accountability, with which the remainder of this study is concerned. The importance of certain public corporations to national development focused a fair amount of public attention on the question of the proper relation of these corporations to the rest of the government. Through this process there came to be a broader recognition of the existence of a class of government agencies known as corporations and of the need to devise measures of dealing with them as a group. At the same time, the relative calm with which Canadians have generally regarded public enterprise has facilitated concentration on the organizational problems without the distraction of viewing these problems primarily through ideological spectacles.

2

The Roots of Accountability

Increasing use of public corporations in democratic countries has brought in its wake a growing awareness of the difficulty of devising an acceptable form of control. An early faith in the theory of the autonomous government corporation has increasingly given way to a realization that the virtue of corporate flexibility may be balanced by the vice of irresponsibility. Widespread recognition of the problem is reflected in recent studies dealing with a number of different countries and situations.[1]

In parliamentary systems effective control of public corporations has assumed particular prominence because of the tradition of full ministerial and parliamentary responsibility. In view of this honored tradition, it may be thought remarkable that a form of government unit ordinarily associated with the notion of considerable freedom from outside controls should have gained a foothold in Great Britain and the Commonwealth. And yet, the home of the Mother of Parliaments also became the haven, in the years between the world wars, for a number of notably independent public corporations. Furthermore, this innovation owed more to the parties of the right and center than to the Labor Party. The Conservatives and Liberals espoused the corporate device largely on the theory that, if public ownership was inevitable for certain British industries, it was wise to "make it as much like private enterprise as possible." [2] The

26

Labor Party, though a much more ardent believer in public ownership, worried more about the responsiveness of nationalized industries to popular control and therefore at first favored direct departmental administration. Although the Laborites were converted to the corporate device long before they came to power in 1945, it is interesting to note that the corporations they created to run the industries nationalized in the postwar period are less autonomous than the British Broadcasting Corporation and certain other prewar corporations. Even though executive and legislative controls over corporations have thus increased over the years in Great Britain, it is significant as a measure of the power of the idea of corporate autonomy that such controls are still not as great as in the supposedly loose-knit American presidential system.[3]

Turning now to Canada, some resemblance to the British developments may be seen. First of all, the years after World War I saw experimentation with the corporate device for the administration of a large commercial enterprise, the Canadian National Railways. True, only one corporation was involved as against several in Britain. This was offset, however, by the fact that, given the respective governmental sizes, the Canadian undertaking was proportionately much larger, and that it came at a time when there were few precedents on which to rely. As a matter of fact, the Canadian National Railways served as an inspiration for the British Labor Party when, during the twenties, it began to abandon its belief in direct departmental administration of nationalized industries.[4] Secondly, the Canadian situation resembled the British in the sense that the Conservative Party led the move to apply the corporate form to a business enterprise operated by the government. Finally, Canada, like Britain, has gradually imposed greater controls on public corporations.

An understanding of the way in which the question of corporate accountability has been posed in Canada can be greatly facilitated by reference to the pioneering debates in the House of Commons on the relationship of the Canadian National Railways to ministers and to Parliament. Although the C.N.R. was not the first public corporation established by the Canadian government,[5] it was the first to be charged with the operation of a giant business enterprise. Parliamentary realization of the need for permitting operational flexibility, coupled with fear of the consequences for responsible government, gave an unequalled sense of urgency to the debates and lay bare, in its essentials, the dilemma of corporate accountability. Even though various factors limited the value of the debates as a precise precedent, their impact still lingers, as the succeeding chapters will indicate. It seems appropriate, therefore, as a prelude to the later discussion, to review them at some length.

A striking feature of the C.N.R. debates was the tendency of participants to rely on the language of business in visualizing the relation of the corporation to ministers, Parliament, and the people of Canada. In this way accountability was seen as a matter of assuring that the people as shareholders in the new public enterprise retained ultimate control of their property. In using business imagery the politicians did not, of course, lose sight of political realities. They knew that the new corporation faced the unenviable task of creating a working system out of the melange of bankrupt private railroads acquired reluctantly during the war and added to a few government-owned railroads formerly under the management of the Department of Railways and Canals. They knew, too, that the success or failure of the C.N.R. was a matter of great moment to the voters. Although these worries run like a thread through the debates, the "shareholder" approach strongly influenced the vocabulary. It seems fair, then, to divide the discussion into the following questions. (1) As a meeting of shareholders was impractical, who were their authorized representatives? (2) To what information were shareholders entitled? (3) How could control by the shareholders be assured?

The first question arose out of the necessity to appoint a board of directors in 1919. The contention of the Liberal opposition was that Parliament should at least help the Cabinet decide both membership and salary. "We are the shareholders in this Parliament," argued a prominent Liberal. "We hold proxies from the people." [6] The reaction of the Union government, which was largely composed of Conservatives, combined the old and the new in accountability arguments. One Cabinet member laid stress on "the basic . . . principle of our Constitution" that "for each appointment the Governor in Council is responsible to Parliament." [7] By contrast, another justified the Cabinet's exclusive role in appointing and paying the directors as an exercise by the Cabinet of the people's rights as shareholders.[8] It can scarcely be argued that political considerations were absent in some aspects of the Liberal opposition's unsuccessful argument for giving Parliament a voice in the appointment of directors. A scheme to let the opposition name a minority of the directors, as one Liberal proposed,[9] smacks of patronage more than of principle. Even so, the fact that proposals of this kind were made on the grounds of Parliament's right to safeguard the shareholders' property suggests a serious challenge — evident also in the discussion reported below — to a cornerstone of the parliamentary system, the concept of ministerial responsibility.

The second question — that of disclosing information to shareholders — revealed the preoccupation of the government and the opposition with rather opposed business concepts. The government was determined that information should not be disclosed publicly in a way that would impair either the managerial autonomy or the competitive position of the C.N.R. The Liberals, at least while they were in opposition, stressed the necessity of frank disclosure of information to the owners of the business.

The stand of the Union government was prompted by memories of unfortunate experiences with departmental operation of the original government railroads, and by apprehension about operating a much bigger system in competition with a great privately owned rival, the Canadian Pacific. Especially fresh in the minds of government ministers was the endless pulling and hauling that had occurred with respect to the management of the Intercolonial Railway, which had been built for the purposes of joining the Maritime Provinces to Quebec and Ontario. Created for political purposes and operated at a loss in order to encourage trade with the Maritimes, the Intercolonial was fair game for politicians and special interests. Successive cabinet ministers who were responsible for its operation tended to manage it for political advantage.[10] Questions in the House of Commons publicized the most minute details of the railroad's business and thereby affected management decisions.[11] Eventually, to spare the Minister of Railways and Canals some of the constant pressure from "patrons of the road," the Conservative government proposed in 1917 that the Intercolonial be regulated by the Railway Commission, as private railroads were.[12] Adoption of the corporate form for government railroads was partly dictated by a desire to isolate them even more from pressure.

Accustomed to learning details of government railway management almost at will, the House of Commons did not take readily to the concomitants of incorporation, as pictured by Unionist Prime Minister Arthur Meighen, a leading architect of the C.N.R. "The Board of Directors is inde-

pendent of Government control and direction," Meighen
told the House in 1921, "and that being so the Government
from day to day cannot be answerable for details of operation." [13] If these matters were to be disclosed in the same
way as for departmental activities, then, said Meighen, "we
are right back where we were with the Intercolonial; we are
under political control." Some questions about current affairs had been answered, Meighen admitted, "where it
appeared . . . that the answering of them . . . could not preju-
dice the position of the company." [14] The usual guiding
principle, however (as summarized on a later occasion by
a former member of Meighen's cabinet), was that "so soon
as the current business was over and became a matter of the
past, and there could be no possible injury done to management, then parliament had a right to the information." [15]

To reinforce their restrictive stand on information members of the Union Cabinet relied on the example of private
business. They pointed to the report of the C.N.R.'s board
of directors as equivalent to "what the board of directors
of a private system discloses to its shareholders." [16] But,
when the Liberals suggested that shareholders in private
companies might obtain additional information by contact-
ing company offices, the Unionists rejected the analogy on
the ground that not all shareholders in a public corporation
(that is, not all Canadians) could be trusted to use information about prices or other management matters in a dis-
interested manner. [17]

So long as they were out of power, the Liberals staunchly
maintained that shareholders of a public corporation are
entitled to full information about current operations. In
1920, for example, the new Liberal leader, W. L. Mackenzie
King, told the House that "it should be a matter of principle
that there is nothing connected with the properties that the
people of Canada own that the people's representatives in

this Parliament should not have a right to inquire into, not at one particular time, but at all times." [18] This view King embodied in a resolution he introduced during the 1921 session of Parliament. It declared that the House of Commons had an "undoubted right" to all documents "in relation to the management of every department of the public service including the affairs of the Canadian National Railways, whether operating directly under the control of the department, or under corporate form." [19] Alas for consistency, the bold stand enunciated by King did not survive his accession to power in the dying days of 1921. Instead of full disclosure of information to Parliament at all times, the Liberals continued their predecessors' policies without much open acknowledgement of the shift they had made.[20] The formidable responsibility of running a railroad under difficult conditions brought to the Liberals, as it had to the Unionists, a realization of the desirability of restricting the information given to Parliament.

The last, but probably the most basic, question of accountability raised in these early debates was the question of how the stockholders could control the C.N.R. Here again the Unionists acted as innovators, with the Liberals criticizing departures from past practices. The immediate past, with its unsavory history of meddling by politicians in the affairs of government railroads, would be only a memory under a public corporation, the Unionists asserted. Already, patronage had been minimized. "I know that so far as I am concerned I have never been consulted with reference to a single appointment," boasted one Cabinet member, "and I am quite satisfied that is equally true so far as my colleagues are concerned." [21] More positively, the Unionists claimed that successful administration of the railways depended on "the appointment of first-class men of the highest standing in the community, men of such self-respect that they will feel that they will be judged so much by the success of their administration of the system that they will not brook any interference on the part of the government." [22]

A crucial question remained, however, and the Liberals were quick to pounce upon it. In assuring the corporation's freedom from the government of the day, had responsible government been safeguarded? "Politics must exist in public ownership in so far as that involves the fullest possible control by the people," the leader of the Liberal opposition asserted. He warned that "If this proposed organization is put in charge of the railroads owned by Canada, that is the end of our control over them." [23] To the Liberals it was incongruous that the traditional system of accountability to Parliament should be removed "from the men who manage the largest and most important branch of the public service." [24] Departmental administration of government railroads, ridden as it was with patronage, at least had the virtue of being understood by Parliament.[25]

The Unionist defense against this line of attack was to articulate a concept of indirect control that remains a classic defense of corporate autonomy. It was conceded by Sir Thomas White, the Acting Prime Minister, that without the patronage problem "the logical position would be for the Government to administer the system directly . . ." [26] Given the desirability of avoiding "political considerations," however, the Unionist leader confessed that "I do not know of any way in which it can be done consistently with the principle of responsible government other than that suggested here, namely, that the Government should appoint those who are to administer the system, these men to have a free, hand in the administration." [27] The line of accountability was etched more precisely by Prime Minister Meighen in 1921. "While there is corporate management, there remains the answerability and responsibility of the Government for the success of the system. That we cannot dispute. But there is no immediate accountability for the day to day procedure of operation. If there is to be then our officers subject to our direction must operate the road . . ." [28] An organizational mixture was not to be tolerated, in Meighen's view. "Can you have corporate management of the road and departmental financing? Or corporate management and departmental auditing?" he once asked in the House of Commons.[29]

As with the question of furnishing information on management to Parliament, the Liberals, when they came into office, settled the argument by following the precedent of the Unionists. In announcing the creation of a new board of directors as part of a reorganization of the Canadian National Railways, the Liberal Minister of Railways and Canals said: "It is the intention of the Government that the board in the exercise of its several duties and functions shall be free from interference, political or otherwise." [30] When Prime Minister Mackenzie King was sharply criticized in the House because of the activities of the new president of the Railways, he countered with a vigorous statement of indirect control: "When the government asked Sir Henry Thornton to take control of the railroad we gave him — and I in the name of the government gave him — a distinct pledge that he would be entrusted with the management, that he would have a board of directors with whom he would be associated, and that the board and he as president would be given a free hand, and that there would be no interference on the part of the government with the action which they were taking. We told him, however, that we would hold him responsible for the manner in which he conducted the affairs of the system . . ." [31] Turning his attention to the specific action criticized — a complicated financial transaction involving the purchase of a Paris hotel in connection with obtaining premises for publicizing the railroad abroad — King said of Thornton: "He took this action without any knowledge on the part of the government . . . We stand here prepared to support [him] . . . We will judge him as the head of the railway by the manner in which that particular transaction, as well as all other transactions . . . turn out. But while he is president of the Canadian National, and we are representing the people of Canada in this House we propose to give Sir Henry Thornton in this and every other transaction precisely the same degree of latitude and freedom as the shareholders of the Canadian Pacific would give to Mr. Beatty [its president]." [32]

From the account of the C.N.R.'s early history sketched above, it is apparent that the party in power, regardless of its previous views, came to defend strongly a system of corporate accountability quite foreign to that prevailing for ordinary government agencies. Both the manner in which Parliament was given information about the corporation and the manner in which the government of the day assured itself of responsible action by the corporation differed from the traditional practice of parliamentary democracies.

Why should there have been such a strong insistence by the government of the day upon a large measure of corporate autonomy at the expense of the traditional system of accountability? Some of the reasons have already been suggested: (1) a recognition that the country had become alarmed at the amount of political interference in departmental administration of the railroads and at patronage abuses in various areas of government service; [33] (2) a feeling that the vastness of the new public railroad empire precluded administration by a department; and (3) a desire to emulate in so far as possible the freedom enjoyed by the C.N.R.'s successful private competitor, the Canadian Pacific. Probably an underlying reason for favoring consid-

erable corporate autonomy was the hope that this would
shield the party in power from the political consequences of
failure in the operation of the railroads under public ownership. The circumstances under which the government became the owner of a miscellaneous collection of railroads
scarcely encouraged the political leaders to anticipate success. Several additional reasons apparently impelled the
Unionists to create the corporation in the first place. They
believed, first, that there were practical advantages in continuing the same form of business organization that had
operated the railroads under private ownership,[34] and, second, that incorporation would assure greater uniformity of
administration than had existed under departmental supervision of government railroads.[35] Finally, the Unionists were,
by their own testimony, strongly influenced by precedent.
Not only the models furnished by private railroad charters
— although imitation of these was rather slavish [36] — but
also precedents of varying degrees of remoteness from rail-
roading. "In my study of the railway situation," Sir Robert
Borden remarks in his memoirs, "I had been impressed with
the fact that the acquisition of the Suez Canal by the British
Government had been carried out through a corporation." [37]
Closer to home and probably more influential with the Conservatives, who had fathered it and reared it, was the example of a provincial corporation, the Ontario Hydro-Electric
Power Commission.[38]

Vivid as the C.N.R. debates were in displaying a whole
gamut of questions about accountability at an early stage of
corporate development, they did not foster any immediate
trend toward regarding public corporations as a group for
which collective rules should be made. The point can be illustrated by quoting the remark of a member of Parliament
in characterizing the period around the year 1931, a dozen
years after the establishment of the C.N.R., as a time when

"they did not have the problem of what we today refer to as crown corporations. It is true they had the Canadian National Railways, but at that time nobody referred to the Canadian National Railways as a crown corporation." [39] The probable reasons for this state of affairs are not hard to find. The relatively few public corporations established between 1919 and 1931 [40] were not of a size or type to provoke easy comparisons with the C.N.R. nor resort to the business imagery that was so prominent in the earlier discussion. Furthermore, creation of the later corporations did not disrupt any parliamentary habit of interference in administration, as in the case of the railroads, and, in any event, the neutral civil service was beginning to be well enough established to discourage any such interference. In addition, a concern about the role of administration in the modern democratic state, now prevalent in Canada [41] as elsewhere, had then not developed very far, and certainly not to the point where the problem of corporations was regarded as part of this larger concern.

Perhaps an even stronger reason for the slow development of an over-all approach to corporate accountability was the emphasis, noted in the previous chapter, on pragmatic action to meet a succession of problems. The pattern of corporate development in the thirties appears to support this reasoning. Important corporations were established to meet the developmental problems of transcontinental radio and aviation, to administer a central banking system and a network of harbor facilities, and to aid in the marketing of wheat. For some corporations of this era, Parliament had to give special attention to organizational questions because of changes made in the original arrangements under which the corporations were to operate. Thus, the Bank of Canada Act of 1934 was amended in 1936 and 1938 to eliminate any trace of private ownership or control, and the Canadian

Radio Broadcasting Commission of 1932 was replaced by the Canadian Broadcasting Corporation of 1936. Two other corporations, the National Harbors Board and the Canadian Farm Loan Board, were set up for the purpose of altering pre-1931 corporate arrangements. In short, the emphasis placed on public corporations in this decade might have argued for the establishment of some general rules of accountability, but the eyes of ministers and Parliament remained fixed on the goal of meeting separate problems as they arose. The cumulative effect of this approach, however, was to increase Parliament's familiarity with questions of accountability. Whether because of this familiarity or because even the important corporations of the thirties did not conjure up the same image as the C.N.R. had earlier, less emphasis on the shareholder concept was apparent, with the possible exception of the debates on the Bank of Canada.

The stimulus for adoption of a broader view toward corporate accountability appears to have come mainly from the widespread use, during and since World War II, of the species of public corporation known as the Crown company. These public corporations owe their existence to the Companies Act of 1934,[42] a statute originally designed for privately owned corporations. Actually, a predecessor of the act was used for public purposes as early as 1927 when Canadian National (West Indies) Steamships Limited was established as a subsidiary of the C.N.R.,[43] but this action remained unique until the war emergency. In 1940, when the government was faced with the problem of tooling Canadian industry for war, the Department of Munitions and Supply Act of the previous year was amended to authorize the Minister of Munitions and Supply to procure the incorporation of companies under the Companies Act or equivalent provincial companies acts.[44] It may be noted that the British Munitions and Supply Department Act, from which the Canadian Act was copied, made provision for companies.[45] Under the Canadian Act, twenty-eight companies were incorporated during the war, eleven to operate plants and the remainder to carry out supervisory, administrative, and purchasing functions.[46] To those seeking a solution to the urgent question of meeting certain special problems of war production, the Crown companies offered "a way which would avoid those delays which are inevitably associated with any large enterprise, public or private, without the weakening of the principle of ministerial responsibility to parliament."[47] To C. D. Howe, the minister of munitions and supply, the Crown company plan offered an inducement to "men with business responsibilities of their own to give a good deal of their time to the government, in executive positions associated with a form of administration with which they were wholly familiar," and it permitted "the head office [to] be established in a location most convenient to those men whom we wished to attract to the business."[48] To some members of Parliament, on the other hand, the Crown company plan presented grounds for uneasiness.[49] They saw a bewildering array of public corporations springing up without individual statutory authorization and at the discretion of a single powerful minister who directed their activities without much publicity. Although parliamentary uneasiness was somewhat allayed by the promise of swift liquidation of the great bulk of the Crown companies upon war's end, the Liberal government's own plans for peacetime use of Crown companies[50] made the passage of regularizing legislation desirable. The result was the enactment of the Government Companies Operation Act of 1946,[51] which was intended to make the legal and fiscal position of Crown companies more uniform. Although, in practice, the statute was not made applicable by government proclamation to all the Crown companies,[52] it served as an important precedent, for most of its provisions were included in Part VIII of the more broadly based Financial Administration Act of 1951.

Without attempting to review the provisions of the Financial Administration Act at this point, its general significance for the development of corporate accountability may be briefly indicated. First, placing statutory corporations as well as Crown companies within the purview of the Act constituted recognition of the need for some general rules to apply to corporations regardless of origin. Second, reliance on financial controls was apparently viewed as central to a scheme of corporate accountability. Third, the inclusion of corporations in a general statute dealing with all types of administrative agencies indicated an attempt to fit corporations into a larger scheme of fiscal controls. Finally, the Act demonstrated continued recognition of the importance of corporate individuality by providing for (1) classification of corporations into three categories (departmental, agency, and proprietary corporations), together with differentiated treatment for each category; (2) exemption of a half-dozen corporations from the purview of the act; and (3) the superiority of statutes under which corporations were established in cases of conflict with the terms of the act.

The respect for variety among Canadian public corporations that is implicit in the Financial Administration Act as well as the individualized treatment of corporations from the days of the establishment of the C.N.R. onward constitute warnings against easy generalizations about corporate accountability. With full recognition of the difficulties involved, an attempt is made in the succeeding chapters to describe and characterize ministerial and parliamentary controls over corporations and the relation of corporate boards to outside bodies.

3

The Supervisors

Probably the most crucial — and yet the most elusive — element in a system of corporate accountability is the role played by ministers. The very definition of a Crown corporation in the Financial Administration Act as "a corporation that is ultimately accountable, through a Minister, to Parliament for the conduct of its affairs..." [1] reflects both the importance and ambiguity of the position. Ministers serve as a link between corporations and the body to which they are "ultimately accountable," and yet, in the nature of things, ministers can not always be held fully accountable for the activities of corporations in the same fashion as for ordinary administrative activities. How far has Canada gone in assuring ministers of control over corporations? What statutory powers do ministers possess? What considerations guide ministers in dealing with corporations? These are the questions which this chapter seeks to answer.

STATUTORY POWERS OF MINISTERS

If statutory powers assigned to the Governor in Council [2] and the Minister of Finance are included along with those granted to the minister to whom a corporation reports, at least four types of ministerial controls over public corporations may be distinguished. They include appointment and dismissal of members of corporate boards, issuance of ministerial directives, approval or veto of certain corporate actions, and — largely as a supplement to the other powers — requiring information. Not all of these powers are of equal importance nor of equal application to all corporations, but all contribute in some way to the pattern of corporate accountability to ministers.

Appointment and dismissal

Unlike the British nationalized industries, appointments to boards of Canadian public corporations usually are made by the Governor in Council rather than by the minister to whom a corporation reports. The minister, however, usually makes the recommendations. The practice of Council appointment has the virtue, as one observer has noted, of conforming "with the usual practice of permitting the Cabinet, with its carefully balanced regional representation, to exercise the power of veto over the decisions of a single Minister." [3] As might be expected, data are not available to indicate the frequency with which ministerial recommendations have been vetoed.

Most of the departures from the rule of Council appointment to boards are minor. Thus, there are a few instances in which a minister is authorized by statute to appoint directors, but always with the approval of the Governor in Council. Appointment of the directors of the Bank of Canada by the Minister of Finance offers one example.[4] Another is provided by the Central Mortgage and Housing Corporation, one half of whose ten-member board is appointed by the Minister of Public Works with Council approval.[5] Other minor exceptions derive from special situations. The first occurs when it is thought necessary or desirable to include on the board representatives of lower levels of government. In three instances one or more provincial governing bodies share in the appointing power. Of the three members of the

Eastern Rockies Forest and Conservation Board, one is chosen by the Lieutenant Governor in Council of Alberta.[6] Each province that has subscribed $100,000 "to acquire and preserve the great historical battlefields at Quebec" is entitled to have a member on the National Battlefields Commission, whose nucleus consists of five federal appointees.[7] Although the statute establishing the Northern Ontario Pipe Line Crown Corporation in 1956 merely provides for federal appointment of the president and four directors,[8] the province of Ontario, by agreement, now selects two of the directors.[9] Urban representation is authorized in the case of the Federal District Commission, two of whose twenty members are appointed by the cities of Ottawa and Hull.[10] A second type of special situation obtains for certain subsidiary corporations. The most notable is Trans-Canada Air Lines, four members of whose board are chosen by the shareholders (that is, the board of the Canadian National Railways) and three by the Governor in Council.[11] By the terms of the Canadian National-Canadian Pacific Act, the directors of the C.N.R. must make their selections from their own ranks.[12] Under the same authority, the C.N.R. board of directors serves as the board of another subsidiary, Canadian National (West Indies) Steamships Limited. The Industrial Development Bank must, by its statutory authorization, always consist of "those persons as members who for the time being comprise the Board of Directors of the Bank of Canada . . ."[13]

The only major exception to the rule of Council appointment occurs in the case of the ten existing Crown companies.[14] The three statutes currently in force which authorize formation of corporations under the Companies Act of 1934 empower a minister or an existing corporation not only to create Crown companies, with the approval of the Governor in Council, but to exercise sweeping powers over appointment and removal of directors. Thus, the Defence Production Act of 1951 provides:

> 7. (1) The Minister may, if he considers that the carrying out of the purposes or provisions of this Act is likely to be facilitated thereby, with the approval of the Governor in Council procure the incorporation of any one or more corporations for the purpose of undertaking or carrying out any acts or things that the Minister is authorized to undertake or carry out under this Act.
>
> (2) For the purposes of this section, upon the request of the Minister, the Secretary of State of Canada may, by letters patent under his seal of office, grant a charter under Part I of the *Companies Act* constituting such persons as are named by the Minister and any others who may thereafter be appointed by the Minister in their stead or in addition thereto a corporation for any purpose mentioned in subsection (1).
>
> (3) The Minister may remove any members, directors or officers of a corporation incorporated under this section at any time and may appoint others in their stead or may appoint additional persons as members.[15]

Although the other two statutes are not as explicit on appointment and dismissal, they accomplish much the same effect by their clear-cut references to control of any companies that may be created. Under the Atomic Energy Control Act, as amended in 1954, the minister may, with the approval of the Governor in Council, "assume, by transfer of shares or otherwise, the direction and control of any one or more companies . . ."[16] Control over appointments was further assured by a provision which authorizes the minister (or a parent company) to hold all the shares of the company except the qualifying shares of the directors. Comparable powers were given to the National Research Council under the Research Council Act.[17]

Because of the absence of mixed-ownership corporations from the Canadian scene at present, no question of formal extragovernmental participation in the appointive process arises. Two instructive examples from the past suggest that future experiments along this line are not likely.[18]

Although Trans-Canada Air Lines was formed as an entirely government-owned corporation in 1937, this action did not follow the original plan of the Liberal government. According to C. D. Howe, the "father" of the airline:

> The intention of the government had been to unite the strongest transportation interests in Canada to undertake this new venture in transportation, and with that in view I approached the Canadian National Railways, the Canadian Pacific Railway Company, and Canadian Airways, Ltd., the latter being by far the strongest of the air transport companies then operating. These companies were invited to provide the needed capital for, and assume the ownership of, the airline company, the government to assume responsibility for building adequate airports and the necessary communication system. Each of the three component companies was to share equally in the ownership of the air line, and each was to have two directors on a board of nine, the government to appoint three directors on account of its investment in airports and communications. . . .
>
> The Canadian Pacific Railway Company and Canadian Airways objected to having three government directors on the board, and at the last moment these two companies withdrew their support, with the result that the Trans-Canada Air Lines Act provided for full ownership of the enterprise by Canadian National Railways.[19]

It appears likely that the two private companies may have feared a 5–4 alignment against them on the board. In another, more famous, case an arrangement whereby private groups controlled the appointing process actually was put into effect. When the Bank of Canada was created in 1934 as a privately owned "public trust," the shareholders were empowered to choose the directors for five-year terms "at annual general meetings." [20] The actual process of election of directors by shareholders led to an unanticipated and, to the Liberal government, "intolerable" result. In the indig-

nant language of Minister of Finance Charles A. Dunning
when requesting a change in the ownership of the Bank in
1936: "Seven directors were to be elected by an unorgan-
ized group of over 12,000 shareholders scattered throughout
the whole of Canada. . . . What in fact happened . . . was
that the Canadian Chamber of Commerce . . . intervened in
the election and submitted a slate of nominees bearing its
recommendations. The result was that every nominee of this
slate was elected. . . . What I am . . . criticizing most se-
verely, is legislation which in practice permits a private
business association in effect to name the directors of our
central bank." [21] What the amendments of 1936 intended
to accomplish was "an actual investment by the country in
excess of the investment of private investors, thus justify-
ing the government in assuming complete control of the
institution by majority control and ownership." [22] Only two
years later the Liberal government requested Parliament to
pass an act authorizing the purchase of all privately owned
shares, giving as the reason that "Doubt has been and is being cast upon the control of the bank by the government
through a majority of the board of directors. This doubt it is
proposed to remove altogether by purchasing the privately
owned stock entirely, so that the people of Canada may
know beyond peradventure that the whole of their national
central bank is owned by the government of Canada." [23]

In detailing the number of appointments to be made to
corporate boards, a half-dozen statutes have permitted vary-
ing degrees of flexibility. Thus, it was theoretically possible
to appoint from five to nine members to the boards of the
National Gallery of Canada and the Canadian Commercial
Corporation, from three to five members to the Canadian
Farm Loan Board, not more than six to the Fisheries Prices
Support Board, not less than six to the board of the Crown
Assets Disposal Corporation, and up to four nongovernmen-

tal members to the board of the Export Credits Insurance Corporation. Although it might be argued that provisions for flexible size facilitate ministerial control over boards, there is no evidence to indicate that this was the motive nor that these particular statutory clauses have been used for such a purpose.

Causes for dismissal of board members range widely from corporation to corporation. Crown company directors serve completely at the minister's pleasure. The same arrangement (except for the substitution of the Governor in Council for the minister) is found in the case of the Canadian Commercial Corporation, whose operations are coordinated rather closely with several Crown companies. The following selected excerpts indicate how statutory provisions run the gamut toward increasingly secure tenure until, with the Canadian Wheat Board, tenure provisions analogous to those possessed by members of the judiciary are reached.

The Governor in Council may, without cause, remove a director at any time during his term [of three years]. [Crown Assets Disposal Corporation]

. . . hold office during pleasure for a period not exceeding five years. [Federal District Commission]

. . . be appointed . . . for a term not exceeding three years, but . . . may at any time be removed for cause. [Canadian National Railways]

. . . hold office during good behaviour for five years. [Canadian Maritime Commission]

Each member holds office during good behaviour but may be removed for cause at any time . . . [Canadian Wheat Board]

For several corporations the tenure of the head or heads of the Board is at least double that of the other members. This is the situation in the Bank of Canada, Canadian Broadcasting Corporation (but in the 1958 statute the longer term is "during pleasure" only), Canadian Overseas Telecommunication Corporation, and Unemployment Insurance Commission. Occasionally, the statutes empower the Governor in Council to fix the tenure of some (National Research Council) or all (Canadian Farm Loan Board) of the directors. Tenure is apparently left to the discretion of the Governor in Council where statutes make no mention of the matter, as in the cases of the St. Lawrence Seaway Authority and the Trans-Canada Air Lines.

Given the usual piecemeal treatment of corporations in Canada, generalizations about the significance of the extreme variations in tenure provisions are somewhat hazardous. Broadly speaking, it may be said that the differences reflect variations in the degree of corporate autonomy. The highly uncertain tenure of Crown company directors appears to be only part of a broader arrangement for ministerial dominance of this type of corporation. Similarly, statutes governing the "departmental" class of corporations usually favor service of board members "at pleasure." The remaining corporations — non-Crown companies in the agency and proprietary groups — tend to have provisions for more secure tenure applied to them, although the pattern is far from uniform. In the apparent emphasis upon tailoring tenure to degrees of corporate autonomy, it would seem that the question of whether there is an ideal length of service for appointees has been largely ignored. Parliamentary discussions appear to furnish few clues on this point. The matter is not perhaps crucial unless service "at pleasure" means in practice frequent dismissals, and it must be said that a comparison of the rosters of corporate boards over the years indicates that turnover has borne little relation to tenure provisions.

Ministerial directives

Although the statutory power to issue directions to corporations is not yet widespread enough in Canada to be said to be "at the crux of ministerial control," [24] as in the British nationalized industries, it represents a development of increasing importance. At least six examples, varying somewhat in their character, may be cited. The earliest is found in the Surplus Crown Assets Act of 1944,[25] which established the War Assets Corporation, predecessor of the present Crown Assets Disposal Corporation. In Section 10 is found the statement, "The Corporation shall be responsible to, and be subject to the direction and control of, the Minister." This is supplemented by the authority in Section 12 that "Subject to general or specific instructions given by the Minister, the corporation may, when so directed by the Minister," perform a series of tasks.[26] The next examples in point of time, the Canadian Commercial Corporation Act and the Atomic Energy Control Act, both enacted in 1946, contain a phrasing of the directive power that more nearly furnished a model for subsequent statutes. Section 4 of the former statute reads as follows: "The Corporation shall comply with any general or special direction given by the Governor in Council or the Minister with reference to carrying out its purposes." [27] With minor variations, this is the wording found as well in the Northwest Territories Power Commission Act of 1948, Canadian Overseas Telecommunication Act of 1949, and the 1951 amendment to the Central Mortgage and Housing Corporation Act.[28]

Both the wording of the directive power and the probable reasons for its inclusion in statutes indicate that the British nationalization statutes did not serve as models, at least in any very specific sense. Significant variations in the wording of the Canadian statutes are, first, the inclusion of the Governor in Council as well as the minister as a source of directive power in every case but one (for which there is a logical explanation),[29] and, second, authorization of the power to issue special as well as general directions.[30] Such information as is available indicates that factors indigenous to each corporation's situation have governed the introduction and use of the directive power. In the case of the Central Mortgage and Housing Corporation, a desire to strengthen government control of housing policy apparently was the motive for adding the directive power to the original statute. When the amendment was being debated, the Minister of Resources and Development made the following statement.

As the hon. member knows, under an arrangement with Defence Construction Limited made recently, Central Mortgage and Housing Corporation is embarking on a broader program of construction operations. Therefore it was deemed advisable, in order that there should be no question of reporting to parliament or of the minister's responsibilities to parliament, that this section should be put into the act to make it quite clear that on matters of policy, and in fact to the extent defined by this section, the minister or the governor in council shall have direct control over the operations of Central Mortgage and Housing Corporation.[31]

As gleaned from interviews with officials in 1956, the experiences of the Crown Assets Disposal Corporation and the Canadian Commercial Corporation demonstrate the variety that may occur in utilization of ministerial directives even among corporations that report to the same minister. In the case of the former corporation, the original reason for inclusion of the empowering clause seems to have been forgotten and the directive power has fallen into disuse. By contrast, the directive power has been used in the case of Canadian Commercial Corporation to expedite action under the organic statute and even to empower the corporation to perform tasks not covered in statute. On occasion the initiative for the issuance of directives has come, not from the Minister of Defence Production, but from the corporation itself.[32]

Although the history of the directive power related above appears to point toward continued (though spasmodic) use of this form of ministerial control, it sheds little light on the criteria for placing such a clause in statutes. The corporations now subject to the directive power appear to have no single common denominator, except that none is a Crown company, a species of public corporation already likely to be under the close supervision of a minister.[33] Not only do the reasons for the inclusion of the power in statutes appear to vary, but the occasion and frequency of use of the power appear to differ widely, on the basis of such information as is available.[34] Finally, it must be noted that since the first parliamentary session of 1951 there have been no new grants of the directive power, even in the two statutes setting up new corporations.[35] Nevertheless, through the precedents already established, there is sufficient awareness of the directive power in Canadian governmental circles to assure its continued authorization on a piecemeal, if rather unpredictable, basis.

Approval of corporate action

The form of ministerial control that has received the greatest amount of systematic attention is the power to approve corporate action. This power rests mainly upon fiscal controls. Part VIII of the Financial Administration Act sets forth a kind of minimum expectation of corporate behavior while avoiding a blunderbuss approach. Departmental corporations, whose financial behavior has all the characteristics of government departments, were excluded from the operation of Part VIII, as were six unclassified corporations whose individuality was considered sufficient to permit them to continue operating wholly under their organic statutes.[36] In

Table 1. Responsibilities of the minister to whom an agency or proprietary corporation reports, the Minister of Finance, and the Governor in Council, under Part VIII of the Financial Administration Act.*

Subject	Minister	Minister of Finance	Governor in Council
Operating budgets (of agency corporations only). Sec. 80 (1)	Receives and approves budgets	Approves budgets	
Capital budgets. Sec. 80 (2)	Recommends approval by Governor in Council; lays approved budget before Parliament	Recommends approval by Governor in Council	Approves budgets
Form in which budgets are prepared. Sec. 80 (3)	May jointly recommend that Treasury Board prescribes form		
Maintenance of bank account(s). Sec. 81 (1)		Approves establishment of accounts and choice of banks	
Creation of special account in corporation's name in Consolidated Revenue Fund. Sec. 81 (2)	Concurs in direction	May direct payment of all or part of corporation's money to account; may pay out this money for corporate purposes or to repay corporation	
Reduction of cash reserves. Sec. 81 (3)	May jointly direct payment to the Receiver General of an amount considered to be in excess of needs; this may be applied toward reduction of corporate debt or as revenues of Canada		Approves direction

* Source: Adapted from *Statutes of Canada,* 15–16 Geo. VI, c. 12 (1951).

Subject	Minister	Minister of Finance	Governor in Council
Loan of working capital (up to $500,000 for each corp.) from Consolidated Revenue Fund. Sec. 82	May request loan of 12 months or less duration	Makes loan; reports every loan to Parliament within 15 days	Approves request for loan
Contractual commitments of agency corporations. Sec. 83			May make regulations as to conditions
Provision for reserves for depreciation of assets, etc. Sec 84	May jointly recommend action		Authorizes action
Preparation of annual statements of account. Sec. 85	May jointly give directions as to form of statements of account listed in Sec. 85 (1) and of such other financial information as either minister may require		

addition, the act provides that in the event of inconsistency between the provisions of Part VIII and the special statutes under which the various agency and proprietary corporations operate, the latter will prevail. Table 1 indicates the nature of the financial controls imposed upon agency and proprietary corporations by Part VIII, as well as the powers given to the ministers to whom corporations report, the Minister of Finance, and the Governor in Council.

When viewed in relation to special statutes, the provisions of the Financial Administration Act may in some cases fill in gaps or, by contrast, provide only minimum direction where the statutes have been quite specific. In either case, the act probably provides some clue to what government circles consider important in the fiscal supervision of corporations. On the broad outlines of financial control it is apparent that the act leaves little to chance. It is very specific on the contents of reports made by auditors and on the necessity of annual reports to the appropriate minister.[37] It is specific, too, on the content of statements of accounts kept by corporations. Only two special statutes require any review of operating budgets of agency corporations;[38] the act not only extends review to all corporations in this category but provides for review by the Minister of Finance as well as the appropriate minister. Section 79 sets the calendar year as the financial year for corporations unless the Governor in Council provides otherwise.[39] In one case, the appointment of auditors, the act even departs from the rule that in cases of conflict the special statutes shall prevail. Section 77 (2) states: "Notwithstanding any other Act, the Auditor General is eligible to be appointed the auditor, or a joint auditor, of a Crown corporation." Even though the act conventionally yields to special statutes, general directions have been virtually omitted in certain areas, such as corporate financing. On this subject, the act merely provides for temporary loans of working capital to corporations, a provision said to be "intended only as an emergency measure to meet urgent and unforeseen requirements, for Parliament has made other provisions for the major financing requirements of the corporations." [40] The act also ignores the matter of investment in securities of money temporarily in excess of a corporation's current needs, a subject covered by numerous special statutes. Even slight mention of a topic in the act may have implications for control of corporations, however. The provision empowering the Minister of Finance and the appropriate minister to require a corporation to pay excess funds to the Receiver General must yield to different arrangements in a number of special statutes,[41] up to 1954 had not been used, and is probably intended only for exceptional circumstances.[42] Yet, as has been pointed out, "paradoxically, its very presence may obviate the need for its use." [43]

The emphasis given the Financial Administration Act in this discussion should not obscure the fact that special statutes undoubtedly can serve as more precise instruments for cataloguing corporate actions that require outside approval. The St. Lawrence Seaway Authority, for example, must have the approval of the Governor in Council for its by-laws, short-term loans, acquisition of lands, leasing of lands to others, and regulations for the management of property.[44] For the Canadian Broadcasting Corporation the Governor in Council must approve leases enduring for a period exceeding five years and involving an amount greater than $100,-000, agreements involving expenditures of $100,000 or more, and the acquisition or disposal of real or personal property for sums exceeding the same amount.[45] What the Financial Administration Act does, in short, is to establish minimum standards of financial behavior for corporations whose origin was not in special statutes (the Crown companies), to round out a system of financial controls for all corporations, and, in effect, to advance some general concepts about the proper relationship of ministers to corporations.

Requiring information

The special statutes customarily require annual reports of corporations, although few are as explicit as the Financial Administration Act both on this point and in requiring the furnishing of additional information. The act details the statements of accounts that, with the auditor's report, must be included in an annual report. Unlike most special statutes, the act also stipulates (in Section 85 [4]) that "A corporation shall make to the appropriate Minister such reports of its financial affairs as he requires."

Some ambiguity about the power of ministers to require information may be introduced by the wording in several special statutes that corporations shall make their annual report *to* Parliament *through* the minister. (The more usual requirement is that corporations submit annual reports to ministers, who in turn lay them before Parliament.) Where the minister is empowered to prescribe the form of the report that goes to Parliament through his hands, the arrangement that held for the Canadian Broadcasting Corporation before 1958,[46] it appears that he would still retain considerable discretion about requiring information. Yet, the requirement of reporting to Parliament may partly account for a statement such as that of the Liberal Minister of National Revenue in 1955: "Because of the nature of broadcasting the C.B.C. has been placed by statute in a position in which it is not responsible to a minister of the crown in carrying out its activities." [47] The Canadian National Railways not only is required to report to Parliament, but the Canadian National-Canadian Pacific Act describes the contents of the annual report in considerable detail.[48] The role of the Minister of Transport is far from negligible, however. In addition to receiving and transmitting the annual reports of the Board of Directors and the auditors,[49] he may, by the terms of the Canadian National Railways Act, "appoint or direct any person to enquire into and report upon any matters or things relating to or affecting the Company or its works and undertakings . . ." [50] He also receives the annual C.N.R. budget, which is then passed on by the Governor in Council before it is submitted to Parliament.[51] A third example of making annual reports to Parliament rather than to the minister involves Trans-Canada Air Lines. The organic statute, however, by stating that the annual report shall include such information "as may be required from time to time by the Governor in Council," clearly indicates that the requirement on reporting does not prevent ministerial acquisition of information. Leaving aside the possible difficulties posed by the foregoing statutes, there are many reasons why any corporation would ordinarily comply with ministerial requests for information whenever made.

The existence of the four types of statutory powers described in these pages gives evidence of an intent to equip the minister to whom a corporation reports, the Minister of Finance, and the Governor in Council with authority to keep a watchful eye on the activities of public corporations. In particular, the powers granted in the Financial Administration Act, when coupled with the various powers given in special statutes, create the impression that the government of the day is far from helpless in supervising corporate operations. Statutes by themselves, however, rarely offer a complete picture. This is true particularly for the relations between corporations and the ministers to whom they report, which are affected by many complex factors. To articulate some of these is the object of the next section.

WORKING RELATIONSHIPS

In considering working relationships between ministers and corporations it will be of assistance to make clear at the outset the degrees of corporate independence from ministerial direction implicit in the three-fold classification of corporations in the Financial Administration Act. The act's intention on this point, as described by a federal administrator involved in its evolution, is as follows for each corporate category.

[Departmental corporations] are subject to the day-to-day directions and control of a minister . . .
. . . Like departments and departmental corporations [agency corporations] are subject to a considerable degree of ministerial

control, but it is perhaps possible to differentiate between the two groups by considering whether the minister's relationship to them is more nearly that of master and servant or principal and agent. Although no very clean-cut line of division can be made it would seem that a distinction has been drawn between a department as a servant of a minister and a corporation as his agent in the sense that a servant is one over whom the employer reserves the control and direction of the way in which the work is to be done and an agent is one who acts on behalf of a principal within the framework of broad directives. . . .

. . . [Proprietary corporations] are usually given a considerable degree of managerial freedom, such control as is exercised by the minister or the Governor in Council being comparable to that of a shareholder who holds all or a major part of the equity stock of a private corporation. For such companies, while a minister (sometimes subject to the approval of the Governor in Council) is usually authorized by Parliament to exercise the equity stockholders' rights of appointing and dismissing the directors and of requiring periodic reports or evidence of satisfactory performance, as in the United Kingdom he is not usually held responsible for the day-to-day acts of the servants of the corporation as he is for the acts of the officers of the department over which he presides. However, to preserve a satisfactory measure of public control and accountability there is sometimes a reserved right of intervening if the occasion arises to give advice or directions.[52]

As a rough description of the types of relations between ministers and corporations the above statement serves admirably. The act cannot, however, make precise distinctions in a matter as intangible as relations between officials, nor was it intended that it should. Although actual working relations are difficult to discover and harder to generalize about, some of the factors involved may perhaps be identified through examination of the dealings of certain corporations with their ministers.

An initial point to be noted is that for the most autonomous corporations — those in the "proprietary" category, plus several not classified, such as the Bank of Canada and the Canadian Wheat Board — the minister-corporation relation labors constantly under diametrically opposite suspicions, which may be phrased as follows. (1) Is independence really a cloak behind which the government can control corporate affairs? (2) Can responsible government be preserved if corporations are able to prevail against the will of the government? The operation of these dual attitudes in the painful development of relative autonomy for the Canadian National Railways was traced in the preceding chapter. The passing years have seen continued expressions of skepticism about the corporation's independence [53] and annoyance at its occasional unresponsiveness to parliamentary requests for information as relayed through the Minister of Transport.[54] Much the same kind of thinking operates with respect to the Canadian Broadcasting Corporation. Thus, the Minister of National Revenue, to whom the corporation reports, complained several years ago that the Conservatives "keep insinuating that in its operations and programs and regulations, the C.B.C. is under the thumb of the government." [55] The Minister, in turn, somewhat exaggerated the situation by stating, in a phrase already quoted in another connection that "the C.B.C. has been placed by statute in a position in which it is not responsible to a minister of the crown in carrying out its activities [see n. 47, above]."

A second factor affecting working relations is that the framework of institutional arrangements must reflect a concern for keeping corporate autonomy within limits that a system of ministerial responsibility can tolerate. The original Bank of Canada Act, establishing a privately owned public agency without a governmental voice in the selection of directors, apparently exceeded the limits of tolerance. Although Prime Minister R. B. Bennett maintained, in the course of debate on the bill, that "the operation of the bank must be subject to the approval of the government of the day, as to the personnel of its officers and the laws under which it operates," [56] his Minister of Finance frankly conceded that, in a showdown between the government and the bank, "Unquestionably the authority of the governor and the board of directors of the bank would prevail." [57] In a discussion reminiscent of the C.N.R. debates more than a decade earlier, the Conservatives defended the arrangement and accused the Liberals of wishing to substitute "political judgment" for "business judgment." [58] The point was also made by the Prime Minister that, if he appointed the directors of the bank as well as the top officials and then were defeated in an election, Mackenzie King would find it even more difficult to deal with the situation than if the government appointed only the officials.[59] Judging by subsequent events, however, these arguments proved insufficient to answer the ultimate question raised by the Liberal leader: "Are the institutions created by governments to be made so powerful that in the matter of national policies they can regard themselves as wholly beyond the direction of a government, where those policies are the result of the will of the people as expressed by their representatives in Parliament?" [60] In the Bank Act revisions of 1936 and 1938 private ownership and private selection of directors were eliminated. In addition, the post-1938 relation of the bank to the government appears to be built around the premise that in a serious clash over broad policy there is no question but that the bank would have to give way, although it has great leeway short of that point. Perhaps the clearest statement of the situation is that made in 1941 by J. L. Ilsley, then minister of finance:

The monetary policy which the bank carries out . . . must be the government's monetary policy, but the government must leave the carrying out of that policy, the choice of ways and means of executing it, to the management of the bank in whose judgment it has confidence.

. . . Let us suppose, however, that the management of the bank and the government do not see eye to eye in the matter of monetary policy . . . In such a case . . . the government's view will prevail.

. . . It would therefore be necessary for [officials and directors who disagreed] to resign, and they would be replaced by others who were willing to accept responsibility for the type of policy which the government believed to be appropriate.[61]

Praise for this arrangement has come from the management of the bank as well as from ministers. In the words of Graham F. Towers, former governor of the bank, when testifying before the Banking and Commerce Committee:

It would be of no use for us to come before a committee of this kind and say in respect to certain actions which were criticized, we did not like that, but the government wanted us to do it . . . There is no alibi possible for the central bank.

On the other hand, there is no alibi possible for the government, because if government said: well, we disagreed with what the central bank did, but parliament has placed the responsibility on them, so what could we do? the answer obviously is that the administration of the day, supported by a majority in parliament, can always alter the legislation. In fact I doubt whether a disagreement would ever necessitate such a thing, because there are various ways and means by which directors and managers can be got rid of.[62]

An incident during the 1958 election campaign marked one of the very few times there has been a public disagreement between the Minister of Finance and the head of the bank. In his annual report to the Conservative Minister of Finance, the Liberal-appointed governor of the bank, without mentioning any political party by name, stated that the bank had not pursued a "tight money policy" between 1955 and 1957 (when the Liberals were in power).[63] The Minister of Finance immediately made public the report and issued a press release disagreeing flatly with the governor's statement. Although the incident drew considerable attention, there were no subsequent public exchanges between the two officials and, after the crushing Conservative victory, no overt indications that an attempt would be made to oust the governor. It may be noted that the incident afforded only an oblique test of the bank-government relation, however, because the dispute was not over *current* policy.

Probably working against the likelihood of disagreements serious enough to produce the ouster of directors and management is a third factor in working relationships, that is, consultation between ministers and corporations reporting to them. Information on the subject is necessarily spotty.[64] Consultation, as used here, must be a blanket term for a great variety of relations between ministers and corporations, ranging from the purely subordinate status of departmental corporations, at one extreme, to the virtual immunity of the Canadian Broadcasting Corporation from ministerial direction on its broadcasts. Probably the Crown companies can be placed next to departmental corporations in the spectrum. Most have rather specialized, often routine tasks that they are expected to fulfill. The prevailing arrangement seems to be that numerous reports are made to the appropriate minister or deputy minister, and it is expected that the officials of the Crown companies will take the initiative to advise ministers of the unusual. This system was apparently in effect in the case of corporations reporting to C. D. Howe in one of his capacities, and its smooth operation may be traced in part to the presence of his trusted lieutenants at the head of many of the Crown companies that reported to him when the Liberals were in office. Even so, close consultation has not been a uniform rule, for in the case of Polymer — a Crown company with the most purely commercial of tasks (the manufacture and sale of synthetic rubber and the products thereof) as well as a location distant from Ottawa — consultation is said to have been rare and to have had a rather different character. At a minimum, however, the role of a minister in consulting with Crown companies (or, for that matter, with virtually all corporations) is probably summed up accurately in an answer given by the Deputy Minister of Finance to a question raised in the Public Accounts Committee:

Q. . . . Is the responsibility of deciding as to whether insurance will be carried entirely with the board of directors of these crown corporations, or is there any residue of responsibility on the part of the ministers of the departments to which those corporations report. . . ?

. . . A. The responsibility rests, in the first instance, with the board of directors of each individual corporation . . . The minister to whom they report has a responsibility to parliament for the proper and sensible management of the corporation. I would suppose that the minister, certainly, has a right to refer this matter back to the board of directors and ask them to reconsider it, if he thinks, in his judgment, that the policy they are following is of doubtful wisdom.[65]

Undoubtedly the most difficult consultative relation to understand is that between the Bank of Canada and the Department of Finance. The difficulty begins with the fact that, by law, the bank operates on its own initiative in certain areas but is purely the agent of the Minister of Finance in others. In its capacity as "fiscal agent of the Government of Canada" as well as "agent for the Government of Canada . . . in respect of the management of the public debt of Canada," [66] there is naturally great need for close and continuous consultation. In its third main function, the management of monetary policy, the bank is not the agent of the government; nevertheless, as we have seen, the government can not permit the broad outlines of monetary policy to deviate from its own notions of what that policy should be and the bank must, as a consequence, give way when the issue is joined. Even when the bank is not acting as an agent, then, consultation plays an indispensable role. In the process, however, the question of whether the bank retains any initiative and individuality comes to the fore. The answer, in part, at least, has been delineated in testimony before the Banking and Commerce Committee. In his appearance before the committee in 1954, Graham F. Towers, then governor of the bank, gave considerable weight to the government's part in consultation, by pointing out that "The government, of course, either through the Deputy Minister of Finance, who is a member of the board and of the executive committee, or through quite frequent conversations between the governor and the Minister of Finance, is always aware of what the Bank of Canada is doing." [67] The practical consequences of this arrangement were depicted by the governor in the exchange that followed:

Q. For instance, in 1948 and in 1951, when you urged the chartered banks to restrict credit, was that advice given without the government first having been consulted by you? A. The government would be aware that we were going to have the conversations. They would be aware, at least through the deputy minister.

Q. And having offered no objection, I suppose one could say they were parties to it, at least in the sense that they did not interfere? A. Yes, because automatically, indeed, they must be parties to everything the central bank does unless they signify to the contrary.[68]

Two years later, in 1956, J. E. Coyne, the new governor, when asked to comment on his predecessor's statements, used the occasion to emphasize another side of the consultation process. He asserted that "... normally I think you would expect the bank to take the initiative in matters which properly fall within its own sphere. The bank is not in the position of daily receiving instructions — or indeed receiving instructions at all — from the government in those matters which by statute are assigned to the responsibility of the management of the bank." [69] If the government took a position on monetary policy that contradicted the bank's views on the subject, ". . . the governor could not and would not react to this difference in view simply by saying: 'Oh, very well, if that is what you want we will do it.' I think there would be a long period of discussion before such a serious difference of opinion would arise, and still further discussion before it would come to a head." [70] Undoubtedly, in discussions the primary source of the bank's strength is its expertise, and, according to the testimony of a former Minister of Finance before the same committee in 1954, it is not lightly overridden. [71] In practice, the differences in working relations produced by dividing responsibility for a whole range of fiscal affairs between the bank and the Department of Finance have been a source of considerable frustration for the opposition in Parliament. In 1956, for example, the Conservatives tried in vain to make government spokesmen state whether they approved of an increase in interest rates announced by the Bank of Canada. Prime Minister Louis St. Laurent would say only that "The government knows the reasons that the governor of the bank had for making that decision. Those reasons were communicated to us and we believe that they are the best judgment of the governor of the bank founded on his research and the information at his disposal." [72] This remark, and others in a similar vein, led an opposition spokesman to declare that ". . . the government cannot shed its responsibility for full fiscal policy in the broadest sense of the word, and that must include the actions of the Bank of Canada, even when, in a technical sense, those actions are taken by the governor of the Bank of Canada in the exercise of the powers conferred upon him by the Bank of Canada Act." [73]

Consultation between the government and the Canadian Broadcasting Corporation provides an interesting contrast to the bank's situation. Because of the C.B.C.'s important responsibilities in the sensitive area of free speech, consultation on programming may leave the government vulnerable to charges of censoring opinions expressed on radio or television. When, for example, the C.B.C. failed to hold a scheduled radio discussion of a book critical of Mackenzie King, Conservatives in Parliament speculated that either the government had interfered or the C.B.C. was anticipating government desires in the matter, an even worse alternative, in their opinion.[74] An even stronger reaction was aroused by former Prime Minister St. Laurent's admission that he had written to the chairman of the board of directors of the C.B.C. about the "tone" of some remarks in a broadcast about Canadian foreign policy.[75] Each Cabinet member was asked in the House whether he, too, had made "representations," [76] and the Prime Minister's action was the subject of a debate in the Committee of Supply during which the point was made that the government could not "stand over" the C.B.C.[77] The Minister of National Revenue, who is the normal channel of communication between the government and the corporation, has a particularly difficult task. The course usually taken by J. J. McCann, the incumbent under the Liberals, was to assert that the C.B.C. bore full and independent responsibility for all program decisions.[78] His cautious stand was further outlined when he was asked on one occasion to state the government's opinion of a certain television program. To the questioner's complaint that instead of a direct reply he had been met with the Minister's statement that the corporation "advised" that it knew nothing of the government's opinions, the Minister replied: "Now, I am not in charge of the Canadian Broadcasting Corporation. I have never interfered in its operation [or] in its policies . . . I purposely have seen that the answers are put as they are, that the C.B.C. replies to the questions that are asked, and they take the full responsibility." [79] Consultation between the Minister and the C.B.C. apparently occurred frequently, although the extent to which it dealt with presentation of his personal views on programming is problematical. As the Minister explained to the House of Commons:

> . . . I have the duty to make representations to the Canadian Broadcasting Corporation with reference to any matter . . . I have made those representations as an intermediary and directly. As an intermediary I receive hundreds of letters from people throughout Canada, some of them commending programs and others severely criticizing them. Those are either passed on by my office or I take them up directly. All the conversations I have had with reference to programs and the like have been personal conversations with the chairman of the board, his general manager and his director of programs.
>
> . . . There are very few communications that pass between me and the broadcasting corporation by letter, because I find it much easier to do business by talking to them directly than by having a long series of correspondence. Throughout the years many of the representations which I have made have been not with reference to programs but with reference to business matters such as the buying of sites. I am continually admonishing the C.B.C. that they are too expensive . . .[80]

At the very least, it is clear from the above quotation that even under conditions that argue for the insulation of corporations, consultation is an important factor. Generally speaking, ministers wish to retain the initiative in communication. This point was well expressed by a former Minister of Finance when the Central Mortgage and Housing Corporation was being established under his aegis in 1945. In agreeing with a critic that certain language in the organic statute should be eliminated, he said that the phrase would have made him "merely a conduit pipe in forwarding recommendations from the corporation to the governor in council." [81]

A final factor worthy of brief mention in describing working relationships is the influence of personality. It can, of course, cut across such formal arrangements as the classification of corporations. As in all walks of life, it does not necessarily coincide with formal organizational lines. When, however, a minister to whom corporations report is also a dominant personality, it may be assumed that the normal powers of his office are vastly strengthened. By all testimony, such was the case with C. D. Howe. Not only was he influential because so many of the nondepartmental corporations reported to him in his various capacities, but the record indicates that his reputation for aggressiveness in dealing with corporations outweighed the niceties of corporate classification. Avoiding some of the more extreme utterances, the conclusion still emerges that over the years his fellow legislators had reason to be impressed with the responsiveness to his wishes of numerous Crown companies, Trans-Canada Air Lines, and even the Canadian National Railways.[82] Similar inferences may be drawn from the informal comments of Crown corporation officials who have worked with him.

CONCLUSION

The data in this chapter suggest that Canadian government corporations, while possessing varying degrees of independence from ministers, do not possess sufficient autonomy to endanger a system of ministerial responsibility. The long arm of the government of the day, it is clear, is capable of reaching into corporate affairs in various adroit ways. The ministers to whom corporations report, the Minister of Finance, and the Cabinet all have important and varied links to the corporations.

Firm control does not appear in this case to mean stultifying rigidity. To a considerable degree, adaptation to the needs of different corporations is assured by the three-fold classification of the Financial Administration Act, by the exemption of certain corporations from its provisions, and by the fact that special statutes take precedence over the act. Flexibility is perhaps more effectively encouraged by the variety of informal factors that inevitably color the working relations of corporations and ministers. Of these, consultation is especially important because it occurs even for the most independent corporations and yet each consultative relation is, for numerous reasons, unique. In general, the primary emphasis in holding corporations accountable to ministers remains on individual treatment. Further generalization must await a glimpse into the way in which public corporations are managed.

4

The Pilots

Ministerial supervision of public corporations, however varied and powerful, need not be restricted to purely external methods. An additional medium for ministerial or departmental influence exists in the composition of the policy-making bodies within corporations. To what extent has this potential tool of accountability been used in Canada? In order to place a question so central to our inquiry in perspective, it is necessary to discuss it in a larger context. What kinds of policy-making bodies pilot the corporations? Next, what forces are represented on the policy-making bodies, either directly or indirectly? Canadian public corporations, closely following business practice, are conventionally headed by boards of directors. The section that follows attempts to categorize these boards and their operating methods.

TYPES OF BOARDS

From an organizational standpoint there are two types of boards among Canadian public corporations, namely, those which merely decide policy and those which, in addition, administer policy. The first category includes the overwhelming majority of corporations. Operating boards, as the second group may be called, are located in a small, but heterogeneous (if one uses the Financial Administration Act classifications) assortment of corporations.

A brief review of the present use made of operating boards should throw some light on the conditions leading to their employment. The two "corporations sole" — the Director of Soldier Settlement and the Director, the Veterans Land Act — constitute, in effect, one-man operating boards. Among the more conventional operating boards, the Canadian Wheat Board and the National Harbors Board stand out for their firm application of the functional principle. Appointments to the five-man Wheat Board are made strictly on the basis of expertise in one skill, the complex business of marketing wheat, while each of the three members of the Harbors Board is an expert on a different matter. The history of these two boards indicates that adherence to the functional idea has not been achieved without difficulty.

The government's move to enlarge the Wheat Board from three members to five in 1953 met with an oblique challenge to the notion of restricting membership to experts in the selling of grain. Opposition critics urged the appointment of representatives of grain producers to the board, arguing that the producers, who owned the grain, should "have a greater hand in determining matters of policy for the selling of grain." [1] In rejecting the plan, the Minister of Trade and Commerce emphasized that the board already sought the opinion of producers via several channels and that ". . . the selling of wheat is itself a highly technical matter . . . I do not think my hon. friend would suggest that we should have a board of five, three with technical knowledge and two without . . . The whole board is not always in one location. We have never appointed to the board a man who has not had years of technical training in the actual selling of the grain, and I would hesitate to change that pattern." [2] Before the National Harbors Board was established in 1936, three-man boards chosen from the immediate locality acted as policy-makers and administrators in each of seven major harbors. When the Liberals came to power in 1935, they abolished the local boards and established a central board at Ottawa composed of three experts in finance, engineering, and business and personnel administration, respectively.[3] The government foresaw a continuation of this arrangement upon passage of the 1936 statute, which was designed, among other things, to make possible the appointment of competent port managers "whose duty it will be to develop the same local contacts that were formerly maintained by the separate harbour boards."[4] Referring to operations under the proposed act, the Minister of Marine stated that "It is not the intention to operate strictly as a board. The thought is more that each phase of harbour engineering will be referred to the member of the board expert in the matter, and that an individual will really be administering a certain phase of harbour work."[5] These words were recalled in the House almost twenty years later when the Liberals sought to add a fourth member to the board, a proposal that produced some statements on the importance of the functional principle as compared with other considerations. Interested members of the House argued fervently that the new board member should be selected from their localities, leading the Minister of Transport to caution his listeners that residence in Ottawa generally loosened the previously close ties to the community from which the new member would be appointed and that, in any event, ability to discharge the statutory duties of the board was a more prominent criterion.[6] Nevertheless, the minister himself, in explaining the operations of the board, indicated that some compromise with the functional principle was necessary. Arguing that selection for expertise was easiest to apply when the board began, he went on to say that in replacing any member the factor of territorial representation inevitably intruded. In addition, "if it had ever been intended there was to be that rigidity in the appointment of members to the board, the statute would have so provided." [7] Finally, the board's experience and the changing times indicated, in the minister's mind, that it might be desirable to represent other skills, such as grain handling and transportation, on the board.

The experience of several other corporations with operating boards is not easily categorized. A sharp decline in the size of the merchant marine has apparently affected adversely the board concept under which the Canadian Maritime Commission began in 1947. In the eyes of the Conservatives, the government permitted its original idea of a full-time, virtually independent commission making vigorous recommendations on the basis of wide consultation throughout the country to degenerate into the reality of "a back-office branch of the Department of Transport." [8] Whatever the true assessment of the situation may be, it is undeniable that the commission does not now have the complete attention of three members, as the statute envisaged. The following developments may be symptomatic of the changed situation: the original chairman, a shipping expert, was succeeded by the Deputy Minister of the Department of Transport, who retained that post while chairman; one of the present members of the commission devotes most of his efforts to his other position as a member of the St. Lawrence Seaway Authority; there has been no haste in replacing another member of the commission, who recently died; and, finally, the present chairman has held five other positions while discharging the duties of his chairmanship! [9] The St. Lawrence Seaway Authority, in its brief span of existence to date, has been an operating board. Following upon this concept, it has no general manager, but the president of the authority is given broad executive powers by statute.

He is labeled the "chief executive officer" and is "charged with the general direction and control of the business of the Authority, and shall have such other powers as may be conferred on him by the by-laws." [10] The organic statute also authorizes the Governor in Council to designate one of the other two members to act in the stead of the president in case of his absence or incapacity, and this member has by administrative regulation been given the title of vice-president. Although the heavy responsibilities of the authority have dictated that the members devote full time to their tasks,[11] it is only the executive officers operating under the authority who possess the needed technical knowledge, unlike the Harbors Board or the Wheat Board. At least one other board beside these two has actually applied the functional principle, but it is now inactive. The tasks of the Fraser Valley Dyking Board, one of the few federal-provincial corporations, occupied the full time of three civil-engineering members during its active period of 1948 to 1950.

The limited experience with operating boards in Canada indicates that they have generally (and understandably) been preferred only for tasks which lend themselves to easy division among the board members. Even so, at an early date there was evidence of some difficulty with the traditional defect of operating boards — coordinated action by the expert members in making policy. A parliamentary committee concluded in 1936 that the Canadian Radio Broadcasting Commission, composed of three commissioners who operated independently in supervising special aspects of policy and administration, had shown "a lack of coordination in dealing with some major questions." [12]

For the second type of board in Canadian public corporations, the policy board, the opposite difficulty has arisen, namely, the question of how to check up on the management of the corporation. This has been true particularly where the board is large, meets rarely, and has mainly part-time members. Canadian thinking on the problem of policy boards has progressed through several stages, as J. E. Hodgetts pointed out almost a decade ago:

In the mid-thirties it was generally assumed that a clear-cut separation could and should be made between those responsible for policy and those responsible for the administration of that policy. For example, when the Canadian Broadcasting Corporation was set up in 1936 a large part-time Board of Governors was presumably put in charge of policy matters, while execution of policy was vested in a General Manager who was not a member of the Board. This separation broke down in practice, for policy issues arose from day to day and had to be determined by the General Manager . . . His decisions were then ratified *ex post facto* by the Board. In 1944–5 the chairman of the Board was made a full-time, permanent official so that he could offset the *de facto* power which the General Manager had come to exercise over policy matters.

The arrangements devised for the Canadian National Railways in 1936 when its board was reorganized illustrate a similar tendency . . . At that time the statute contemplated two separate positions, that of the chairman, who was to be responsible for policy, and that of the President, who was to be responsible for execution and not a member of the Board. In fact . . . the temporary expedient was adopted of appointing one man to hold both posts. This temporary arrangement has been continued.

The Boards of more recent corporations provide stronger evidences of this tendency to bring the chief operating officials to the policy level. In some instances, indeed, the chief operating (executive) officer is not only put on the Board but is made chairman of the Board.[13]

Examination of annual corporate reports and other materials demonstrates that the idea of linking policy and administration on boards — short of actual combination, as in the operating boards — is widely accepted. A common arrangement in the postwar Crown companies, for instance, is for the president to serve also as head of the board of directors. (The President of Eldorado Mining and Refining Limited even has the additional title of "Managing Director.") The emphasis upon combining these functions is not limited to the Crown companies. The Canadian Overseas Telecommunication Corporation Act, for example, provides that "The Board shall consist of a director who shall be the President and General Manager and four other directors." [14] In the corporation's annual reports the president and general manager is also listed as chairman of the board. At the head of the reconstituted Canadian Broadcasting Corporation of 1958 is a president who, as the chief executive officer, presumably will be the leading director, although no provision for a chairman of the board is included in the statute. The Bank of Canada provides an extreme example of vesting responsibility for policy in the person acting both as head of the board and chief executive officer. A brief explanation for the arrangement is found in the testimony of J. E. Coyne, governor of the Bank of Canada, before the Standing Committee on Banking and Commerce:

. . . there is a very special responsibility resting on the governor, who is not only the chairman of the board, but chief executive officer. He has the authority to exercise all of the powers of the bank, unless they be, by the act, reserved specifically to the board of directors. By and large, in the field of ordinary monetary operations, the governor has all the powers of the board of directors. He cannot necessarily overrule them. There are some technical provisions in that regard. If there were ever any dispute between the governor and the board of directors, provision is made for it to be referred to the Minister of Finance and he submits the matter to the governor in council, who has the power to decide it. However that, of course, has never happened, and I trust it never will happen.[15]

Also symbolic of the tendency to provide a closer check

on the implementation of policy is the use of executive committees. As may be expected, their use is authorized mainly for the larger boards, but this is not an infallible guide. The eighteen-member Federal District Commission, for example, has no executive committee, and yet, the chairman of the commission has expressed himself as "quite happy" with the size of the body.[16] Probably a more crucial criterion than size is the degree of flexibility needed by a specific corporation in obtaining frequent authorization for actions. The boards for which executive committees are authorized range in size from the twenty-one members of the National Research Council down to six for the Crown Assets Disposal Corporation. Conventionally, those members of a board who are also officials in the company constitute the core of the executive committee, again indicating the close link between policy-making and policy execution. The powers of an executive committee usually coincide with those of the board from which the committee is chosen, but it is customary to require that committee decisions or minutes of proceedings be reported to the board at its next meeting.[17]

Organizational arrangements for obtaining good liaison between policy-makers and administrators, however elaborate, probably do not tell the whole story. Where boards meet infrequently but decisions must be made daily, it may be suspected that executives avail themselves of opportunities to communicate informally with directors. Some evidence to back up this suspicion is available in public records. When Donald Gordon, president and chairman of the board of directors of the Canadian National Railways, was asked to explain his relation to the seven-man board, he stated that "We have formal meetings once a month. But the board of directors are consulted on matters of policy constantly. I mean they are constantly at my call and I can talk to them by telephone. Occasionally I call two or three of them together as a sort of executive committee. We hold formal board of directors meetings once a month to look after legal details and so on. But in addition to that, the Board of Directors are constantly available to me for their advice and judgment in matters of policy." [18] An allied, but somewhat different, arrangement is suggested in the following exchange between the chairman of the board of governors of the pre-1958 Canadian Broadcasting Corporation and a member of a parliamentary committee:

Q. . . . has anything of a major policy been changed in British Columbia without consulting the governor [that is, member of the board] from that province? A. The board of governors as a whole make all the major decisions.
Q. How often would they meet? A. About once every two months.
Q. If something came up of interest to the people of British Columbia in the period between those meetings, would you consult with the governor from that province? A. Very possibly.[19]

Even though policy boards do not in every situation play a central role in decision-making, the importance of boards to the direction of Canadian public corporations is, in general, undeniable. The composition of boards and the forces that play on them are matters of great moment.

REPRESENTATION ON BOARDS

As each corporation inevitably has some sort of a public, however restricted, the question of reflecting the opinions of the affected group or groups is raised. Most of the usual methods of accomplishing this purpose are present on the Canadian scene, though none to an overwhelming degree. In the course of the following pages an attempt will be made to characterize the uses made of an indirect form of representation, the advisory committee, and of direct representation (on boards themselves) from geographical areas, occupations, and government departments.

In view of Canada's great size and the existence of easily definable regional areas, there is a surprising lack of requirements (at least of a formal variety) for territorial representation on corporate boards. Indeed, the size of the country appears to work against the idea when the aim is to obtain a board that can be on call to meet fairly often or one whose members must devote considerable time and thought to problems of the corporation to the exclusion of other activities. The Canadian National Railways offers a notable example of a shift from a very large board chosen along geographical lines to one a third as large and selected for other reasons. Paid only an honorarium, meeting infrequently, and under strong pressure from their home communities, the original board soon encountered criticism for its lack of effective supervision of the activities of the C.N.R. management. Eventually the board was abolished, and, after the railroad had been operated under a receivership for several years, a new board of seven members was created in 1936. The concept under which it was begun, as C. D. Howe, then minister of transport, explained later, was that it "would be large enough to give reasonable representation and small enough so that the directors could be paid a salary and be expected to live where they could attend meetings of the board and give their continuous attention to the affairs of the railroad." [20] Under this arrangement, "geographic considerations have been taken into account" in appointing board members,[21] but continued residence in an area distant from headquarters of the railroad in Montreal has been discouraged. Thus, to a member of the House from British Columbia who wanted a larger and more representative board, Howe commented as follows: "Vancouver no doubt would be very honoured to have a director on the board; but could anyone guarantee that that director would attend the meetings which I believe take place every week? We have a member from Saskatchewan, but in every case the member from Saskatchewan has moved to Montreal and put himself in a position to attend to the business of the board." [22] In the case of Trans-Canada Air Lines, also a seven-member board, much the same reasoning was pursued by Howe, although this time the Liberal government yielded to demands for increasing the size of the board.[23] At the time the minister first announced his willingness to enlarge the board, he pointed out that members had been appointed from the central provinces in the past because the board was unsalaried, and "a man will not travel all the way from Vancouver and lose a week's time for no compensation." [24] Western members of the Committee on Railways and Shipping assured the minister, however, that this was a sacrifice a western appointee should make in the interests of obtaining a more sympathetic approach by the airline toward his region.

As the above examples suggest, members of Parliament have been sensitive to the composition of boards and have not hesitated to make their views known. On occasion, the Canadian Maritime Commission has been the object of a complaint that none of its three members was from either coast, the absence of a representative of agriculture on the board of the Canadian Commercial Corporation has been questioned, and a Conservative lady M.P. has suggested that a woman be added to the existing membership of the Unemployment Insurance Commission.[25]

The relatively few formal provisions for representation on corporate boards exhibit little uniformity. The statutes governing the Federal District Commission and the pre-1958 Canadian Broadcasting Commission emphasize geographical representation. The twenty members authorized for the former body, "shall include one member for each province who shall be ordinarily resident in the Province for which he is appointed," plus two members appointed by the cities of Ottawa and Hull.[26] The eleven-member board of governors of the C.B.C. was "chosen to give representation to the principal geographical divisions of Canada." [27] In making appointments the Governor in Council apparently did not take this wording to mean that each province would be represented at all times, but that there should be regional representation with attention to population distribution. Of the ten members listed in the 1954–55 annual report of the C.B.C., for example, two resided in the Maritimes, five in Quebec or Ontario, and three in the western provinces. The fact that some provinces in eastern or western Canada were not represented at a given time drew occasional protests from spokesmen for the temporarily neglected provinces. Thus, in the hearings conducted by the Special Committee on Broadcasting in 1953, the following exchange took place when A. Davidson Dunton, chairman of the board of governors, was the witness:

Q. There is no one on the board of governors from Alberta? A. No.

Q. I point out that the people of Alberta feel there should be one from Alberta. A. There have been times in the past when there has been one from Alberta and has not been one from other western provinces.[28]

When the witness was asked whether "a governor from a particular province would represent that province's point of view," he stated that he preferred wording to the effect that "he or she would likely have a more intimate knowledge of the problems and points of view in that province." [29] Occupational representation, in some degree at least, is sought by the organic statutes of two other corporations, the

Unemployment Insurance Commission and the Bank of Canada. In the former case the act provides that "One Commissioner, other than the Chief Commissioner, shall be appointed after consultation with organizations representative of workers and the other after consultation with organizations representative of employers." [30] Directors of the Bank of Canada are to be selected "from diversified occupations." [31] Study of the backgrounds of directors listed in the bank's 1955 annual report suggests that this injunction has been followed in so far as various types of business are concerned. Investment houses, insurance companies, large department stores, manufacturers of such diverse materials as heating products, elevators, salt, and tobacco, and companies in mining and fishing were represented on the board. Because most of the bank's directors who held high positions in these companies also were directors of other companies, even more businesses undoubtedly are represented. Outside of the business realm, representation on the board appears to be spotty. A doctor and a lawyer (who was also president of a fire insurance company) were listed among the directors in 1955, but not obvious representatives of labor or agriculture. Several other forms of formal representation on boards of corporations may be mentioned briefly. Representation for the appropriate provinces is assured in the case of such federal-provincial boards as the Eastern Rockies Forest and Conservation Board and the Northern Ontario Pipe Line Crown Corporation, as well as for the National Battlefields Commission, an agency corporation.[32] A balance between "governmental" and "nongovernmental" representation is achieved on the board of the Central Mortgage and Housing Corporation. By law the board is composed of the president and vice-president, three directors from the public service, and five from outside the public service.[33]

Statutes are not, of course, a completely accurate guide to the nature or extent of attempts to obtain representative boards. As we have seen, without statutory direction the composition of the C.N.R. board reveals attention to geographical representation. The five nonpublic service members of the Central Mortgage and Housing Corporation's board are, without statutory request, drawn from a variety of places and occupations. By tradition, the commissioner of the Canadian Farm Loan Board is a westerner. The Bank of Canada's board has relatively balanced territorial representation, although the statute requires only occupational representation. Similarly, there was a conscious attempt to secure broad occupational representation for the board of governors of the C.B.C. even though this was not required by statute.[34] The 1958 statute that reestablished the C.B.C. contained no provision for territorial representation, as the earlier statute had, but the membership of the new board indicates that close attention is being paid to this factor.

As the foregoing discussion indicates, the purpose of territorial representation on boards is quite clear, but there may be some ambiguity about the purpose of functional representation. Is it used primarily to give various groups in the economic order a voice in running a public corporation, or is its chief purpose more clearly tied to obtaining favorable results from the operations of a corporation? Although these purposes are not mutually exclusive, it may be possible to detect leanings in one direction or the other. The broad distribution of occupational affiliations — for example, labor executive, housewife, trust company executive, dean of a faculty of science, stock broker, political scientist — among members of the pre-1958 C.B.C.'s board of governors suggests that a sincere attempt was made to meet the first purpose listed above. The cultural goals of the C.B.C. may well tip the balance here, for in the more purely

business-oriented corporations the main purpose of occupational representation appears to be the achieving of practical results. For example, an emphasis on this goal may
largely explain the restriction of directorships in the Bank
of Canada to business representatives. Again, the example
of some private corporations in having large boards composed of leading businessmen has been cited as a desirable
precedent for the Canadian National Railways on the
grounds that: "First, men with wide experience ought to
be able to offer good judgment and good advice. Second,
men with wide business backgrounds should be able to help
the road get business." [35] Actually, the present medium-
sized C.N.R. board, like that of its subsidiary, Trans-Canada
Airlines, is already staffed with leading businessmen. The
goodly proportion of businessmen on the boards of Crown
companies furnishes another good example of using occupational representation in order to get favorable results from
corporate operations. The following views of C. D. Howe
(the businessman in government par excellence) on the
composition of one of the corporate boards under his control when the Liberals were in power may be taken as typical of the prevailing outlook toward Crown company
boards: "On the directorate of Atomic Energy of Canada
Limited we have placed practical men from industry. There
are four or five men from the large electrical power companies, and one or two others from industry generally. We
hope that as a result of their contact with atomic energy we
will get a directive as to how best to proceed with the practical development of atomic energy." [36] During World War
II the Liberal government did adopt a policy of placing one
union official on the board of each of the numerous companies then created.[37] A trade unionist still sits on the board
of Polymer Corporation Limited, which dates from this era,
but the policy has not been extended to the newer Crown
companies.

The practice of drawing part-time board members from among the officials of private corporations has not drawn a challenge on the ground of a possible conflict of interest, but recently there have been signs of an awakening parliamentary interest in the question as it pertains to full-time Crown company officials. For at least some of the public corporations, the possibility of a conflict of interest is taken care of by specific statutory prohibitions. A portion of the statutory oath sworn by a governor of the pre-1958 Canadian Broadcasting Corporation upon taking office stated that "I will not accept or hold any other office or employment, or have any pecuniary interest, direct or indirect, individually or as a shareholder or partner, or otherwise, in broadcasting or in the manufacture or distribution of radio apparatus." [38] (A comparable statement is in the new statute.) This was interpreted to mean that a representative of the private broadcasters' trade association, the Canadian Association of Radio and Television Broadcasters, may not sit on the board of governors.[39] Statutes governing the Bank of Canada and the Central Mortgage and Housing Corporation also contain restrictions upon permitting board members to have a pecuniary interest in the corresponding private institutions.[40] Although businessmen's part-time service on Crown company boards is not governed by statutory rules, it has been regarded primarily as a free contribution by experts to important units of national defense. In the circumstances no challenge to the policy of having businessmen on the Crown company boards in a part-time capacity seems to have arisen so far. The private business connections of two full-time Crown company officials drew objections in the House of Commons during the 1957 parliamentary session. Prime Minister St. Laurent confessed ignorance of the fact that the managing director of Polymer Corporation Limited was also a director of three private mining companies and that the president of four Crown companies involved in the government's atomic energy effort was also a director of a private investment firm financially interested in uranium mining companies.[41] Although in the former case a direct conflict of interest was not demonstrated and in the latter case personal responsibility for the decision to invest in uranium stocks was disclaimed,[42] the general issue raised by the incidents does not appear to have been settled. Parliamentary alertness to the possibility of a conflict of interest in similar cases does now exist, however, and this awareness is not confined to the Crown companies. In 1956 questions were raised in the House about the possibility that the newly appointed general manager of the Northern Ontario Pipe Line Crown Corporation might be influenced by his directorships in four private companies, two of which had at least a remote connection with the oil industry.[43]

As direct representation of territorial and occupational interest appears to be employed — at least formally — only to a limited extent, it is appropriate to ask whether advisory committees serve as the vehicle for representing these interests. An answer to the question is not so easy to discover as might be supposed. Although statutes have been the basis for establishing most advisory committees, others have come into existence through other means. Whatever the origin of a committee, the use actually made of it is another matter. When these factors are taken into account, it is seen that for only about a third of all public corporations has the device been contemplated, and in only a few of these instances has it been used diligently or imaginatively. The uses made of advisory committees, nevertheless, deserve to be explained at greater length because of the light such information will throw on the relations of some boards with their "constituencies."

Arrangements for the seven corporations (six since August 1958, as the new C.B.C. statute omits mention of advisory committees) empowered by statute to use advisory committees display considerable variety.[44] In five instances the appointment of more than one committee per corporation is authorized, but two statutes stipulate that only one should be appointed and fix the maximum size.[45] In two instances the composition of the membership is specified. The Canadian Wheat Board Act states that six members shall be "representative wheat producers." The advisory committee under the newly established Agricultural Stabilization Board (which replaces the Agricultural Prices Support Board) consists of "a chairman and at least six, but not more than nine, other members, composed of farmers and representatives of farm organizations." [46] The methods of appointment of committees range from the complete freedom of appointment given the pre-1958 Canadian Broadcasting Corporation to appointment by the Governor in Council in the case of the Canadian Wheat Board and the Export Credits Insurance Corporation. In between are arrangements for ministerial appointments and for having the corporate board appoint committees "with the approval of the minister" or "in accordance with regulations made by the Governor in Council."

Statutory authorization does not appear to be nearly so important a criterion for the use of advisory committees, however, as the operating necessities of particular corporations. Some of the statutory provisions for advisory committees have not been put into force or have been allowed to languish after an auspicious beginning. Thus, advisory committees are not now active in the case of the Canadian Maritime Commission, Dominion Coal Board, and Fisheries Prices Support Board. The most extreme example of nonuse may well be that of the Canadian Farm Loan Board. The original statute of 1935 provided for the creation of local loan advisory boards in provinces where the board was authorized to make loans.[47] No action was ever taken on the basis of this provision, and in 1952 it was repealed. In its place was inserted a provision authorizing the appointment of a "Canadian Farm Loan Advisory Board" consisting of five to ten members.[48] Once again the pattern was repeated; no appointments were made and the section was finally repealed in 1956.[49] By contrast with the foregoing, four corporations use their statutory advisory committees on a more or less systematic basis. The most elaborate system of consultation was established by the Canadian Broadcasting Corporation under an injunction in the 1936 statute to set up "advisory councils to advise it as to programs." [50] Programming in the fields of religion, education, and civic affairs has depended to a considerable degree on the decisions reached by the several advisory councils. The National Religious Advisory Council, whose members are nominated by their denominations, has been responsible for the allotment on a proportional basis of the free time made available for religious broadcasting. A large and representative committee, the National Advisory Council of School Broadcasting, has advised the C.B.C. on the extensive program of radio (and, increasingly, television) broadcasts to school children. A weekly radio and television program on public affairs called "Citizens' Forum" benefits from the advice of an advisory committee selected from the membership of a cross-section of business, labor, and civic groups.[51] Unlike the Canadian Farm Loan Board, the other two corporations connected with agriculture, the Agricultural Stabilization Board (along with its predecessor) and the Canadian Wheat Board, have made regular use of statutory advisory Committees. Spring and fall meetings followed by submission of recommendations appear to have been the procedure of the committee attached to the Agricultural

Prices Support Board.[52] The bill that replaced this board with the Agricultural Stabilization Board was amended on the floor to include a provision that the new advisory committee "shall meet at least twice a year" in order to discharge its important responsibilities of advising on what commodities should be placed under price support and what the support prices should be.[53] In 1944 the House of Commons was told that during the preceding year the Canadian Wheat Board's advisory committee met four times (twice in the grain belt area) and that each time the committee met with officers of the board.[54] A decade later, on the other hand, it was reported that only one meeting of the advisory committee was held.[55] An annual meeting of the advisory committee is also the custom in the Export Credits Insurance Corporation, whose annual report for 1956 credits the "Advisory Council" with a change in the way income from premiums is treated in the accounts. Aside from the comprehensive review which this council gives to the Corporation's activities, individual council members are frequently called upon during the year for advice on a problem with which their background makes them familiar.[56]

Further indications of the virtual irrelevance of statutory authorization for advisory committees may be found in the existence of several busy nonstatutory committees. After World War II, when the Federal District Commission was given increased responsibilities in connection with the development of the Ottawa area, the commission appointed a National Capital Planning Committee to assist it. The committee was "composed of eminent Canadian architects, engineers, townplanners, and representatives of the municipalities concerned," whose duty it was to act as the commission's "permanent advisory body on the preparation and implementation of the Master Plan." [57] It is interesting to note that, after the province of Ontario had created an

Ottawa Planning Area Board, a situation existed whereby "the memberships of the Federal District Commission, the National Capital Planning Committee and the Ottawa Planning Area Board are interlocking, while the technical advisers of all three bodies work in close cooperation." [58] Several other corporations appear to employ variations of the advisory committee system. At any one time, twenty-five to thirty "Associate Committees" operate under the National Research Council — which itself was once an advisory body and still bears the title in its full name.[59] The associate committee mechanism was employed almost from the time the N.R.C. was established in 1917. The procedure is as follows: "When a main problem arises the Council calls together all the leading persons in Canada who are working on the problem or who are particularly qualified to offer advice because of special training or experience. Their first duty is to review the present state of knowledge on that problem both in Canada and abroad. They then draft a specific research program for Canada." [60] The departure from normal advisory committee functions can be seen in the fact that "The Council looks after the administrative details; the committee outlines the researches, recommends the laboratory in Canada in which they should be conducted, and assesses the merits of the results." [61] Although Atomic Energy of Canada Limited has an Advisory Committee on Atomic Power, its primary function is not to advise the corporation but to acquaint Canadian electric power companies with progress in the development of atomic power and thereby to enable them to "evaluate the economic significance of the project in terms of their respective power requirements." [62]

Attachment to the term "advisory committee" should not be made into a fetish, of course; even where a corporation is not using advisory committees, informal or indirect contact with appropriate private groups may be established or at least be available in case communication becomes desirable. Thus, although Canadian Arsenals Limited has no advisory committees, it has access to various industry committees which are coordinated through the Canadian Industrial Preparedness Association. The Canadian Maritime Commission, which has the statutory power to establish advisory committees, ordinarily prefers to meet on a more informal basis with directors of shipowners' and shipbuilders' associations. Despite the scanty use of actual advisory committees, the commission's present chairman deems possession of the power to create such committees when needed a useful tool to have in reserve. The Fisheries Prices Support Board abandoned an elaborate system of advisory committees in 1949, two years after establishment, because "it became apparent that the members of the Board themselves were sufficiently familiar with all details of the various fisheries of the country to enable them to make sound recommendations to the Minister of Fisheries." [63]

Clues to the usefulness of advisory committees are difficult to identify, but, in general, they may be located in the composition of corporate boards, in their operating procedures, and in the history of their dealings with interest groups. More than one of these factors may be involved in a specific situation, as the following examples will demonstrate. Although the Canadian Broadcasting Corporation has had a relatively representative board, it has made broad use of advisory committees, as we have seen, in order to assure itself of adequate programming in areas as sensitive as religion, education, and political affairs. The National Harbors Board offers a sharp contrast. Influenced by the experience of its predecessors, the local harbor boards, with strong community pressure and by its own practice of holding open hearings in the various ports, the board has resisted attempts to represent interests among its membership and to establish local advisory committees.[64] While the affected interests were also denied seats on the Canadian Wheat Board, as previously noted, a fruitful relation with grain producers was established through the use of an advisory committee. In this connection it is pertinent to note that in 1944 Minister of Agriculture J. G. Gardiner reported to the House that the Canadian Farm Federation, given a choice between membership on a wartime food board or representation on an advisory committee, had chosen the latter.[65] In proposing such a committee for the Agricultural Prices Support Board, then in process of being established, the Minister made out the most persuasive case for advisory committees to be found in the annals of Parliament:

> When a producer has been on a board . . . for two or three years he ceases to represent the producers. . . .
> In addition I do not believe that anyone who is in the pay of the government . . . is nearly as free to criticize the government . . . and so I believe the producers are in a much stronger position when they have adequate representation on an advisory committee . . . While . . . the advice is given just as the advice of officials is given to the government, yet these men are free to go back and advise their own people and give them the reasons why certain things are not being or are being done, and their own organizations are perfectly free to criticize the government for anything which the government has decided to do after considering the advice given to them by the committee.[66]

To these points can be added two others involving procedure which, according to an official of the Department of Agriculture, have been vital to the success of the advisory committee associated with the former Agricultural Prices Support Board: (1) a committee, because it is only advisory, must not be permitted to take formal votes or pass resolutions, but should be kept to the task of finding formulas for action which are generally acceptable; and (2) meetings of officials with an advisory committee should be in secret so that ideas can be freely exchanged or compromised without loss of face.[67]

Without a doubt the most controversial aspect of representation — and yet the most significant in terms of indicating the relation between a corporation and the rest of the government — is the matter of assigning membership on boards to departmental representatives. Canadian practice, unlike British, has been to place senior departmental representatives on the boards of some types of corporations, mainly those engaged in lending, insuring, trading, or an activity associated with national defense. The Department of Finance, for example, has had at least one representative on the boards of seven corporations: the Bank of Canada, Industrial Development Bank, Export Credits Insurance Corporation, Central Mortgage and Housing Corporation, Canadian Farm Loan Board, Northern Canada Power Commission, and Northern Ontario Pipe Line Crown Corporation. The Department of Defence Production has been represented on the boards of the Canadian Commercial Corporation, Defence Construction (1951) Limited, and Crown Assets Disposal Corporation. The Department of National Defence has had representatives on the boards of Canadian Arsenals Limited and Canadian Overseas Telecommunication Corporation. A representative of the Department of Trade and Commerce has sat on the boards of the Canadian Commercial Corporation and Export Credits Insurance Corporation. Viewed from the standpoint of individual corporations, the extreme case is represented by the Canadian Commercial Corporation, whose board members are all departmental officials with the exception of the president. Four of the members of Export Credits Insurance Corporation's seven-member board are from departments.

A listing of purely departmental representatives does not complete the picture of departmental influence through membership on corporate boards, however. A good many of the substantial number of corporations clustered around C. D. Howe in one of his capacities (Minister of Trade and Commerce, Minister of Defence Production, and chairman of the Committee of the Privy Council on Scientific and Industrial Research) have had interlocking directorates. Men associated with the minister when he organized facilities for war production during World War II often filled several portfolios in wartime corporations. This practice was continued after the war and during the cold war buildup. The following summary gives a few outstanding examples of overlapping membership on the part of trusted lieutenants.[68]

W. J. Bennett — president, Atomic Energy of Canada Limited; president, Northern Transportation Company Limited; president and managing director, Eldorado Mining and Refining Limited; president and managing director, Eldorado Aviation Limited.

L. C. Audette — president, Canadian Maritime Commission; president, Park Steamships Limited; director, Crown Assets Disposal Corporation; director, Export Credits Insurance Corporation.

W. D. Low — president, Canadian Commercial Corporation; director, Defence Construction (1951) Limited; director, Crown Assets Disposal Corporation.

When it is considered that departmental representatives also frequently serve on more than one board, an image of strong departmental interest in the doings of corporations becomes even more vivid. By way of example, K. W. Taylor, the deputy minister of finance, has served simultaneously as *ex officio* member of the board of the Bank of Canada and the Industrial Development Bank as well as regular member of the Canadian Farm Loan Board and the Export Credits Insurance Corporation. Two assistant deputy ministers of the

Department of Defence Production have served as directors of both the Canadian Commercial Corporation and Defence Construction (1951) Limited, and one of these officials has been, in addition, vice president and a member of the board of Crown Assets Disposal Corporation.

As the preceding paragraph suggests, senior civil servants are the most likely candidates for departmental representation on corporate boards. Unlike the situation in some Canadian provinces, the political heads of departments do not serve as directors. This is so for reasons both of practicality and propriety, apparently. For one corporation, the Canadian Farm Loan Board, the experiment of placing a minister on the board was actually tried but was abandoned after eight years. The original statute provided that the minister of finance should be the chairman of the four-member board.[69] In 1935 the act was amended to remove the minister from the board, to set up a new board of three to five members, and to place the deputy minister of finance among the membership.[70] In explaining the change, E. N. Rhodes, the Conservative minister of finance, stated:

I can not see that any good purpose will be served by discussing the broader question as to the wisdom of a minister of the crown attempting to preside over a board of this character, but I will say this, that with the demands upon the time of the Minister of Finance it is physically impossible for him to attend to the detailed work of presiding at meetings of the board and dealing with individual instances of loans. It simply cannot be done and as a matter of fact, during the whole period of time in which I have had the honour to occupy the office of Minister of Finance, I have been able to attend only one meeting of the board and that was on an occasion of special significance, having to do with the matter of dealing with general, broad principles.[71]

With a continuing trend toward greater complexity in government, it may be anticipated that on practical grounds alone further experiments along this line will not be under-taken. The wisdom of placing a minister on a board might be questioned on other grounds as well, as C. D. Howe dem-onstrated during debate on the Atomic Energy Control Board Act in 1946: "For example, sitting on a board of five the minister might be overruled and outvoted four to one, which would hardly be consistent with the line of authority. Then if a recommendation came from a board of which the minister was a member and it became the duty of the deputy minister to overrule the decision of the board, or to recommend to the minister that he over-rule that decision, there would be some difficulty. I am strongly of the opinion that the board will function very much better if no minister of the Crown is a member of it." [72] In view of the Minister's suspicion that the lines of authority would be confused if ministers sat on boards, it is interesting to note that the opposite fear has been ex-pressed by a civil servant who has been a member of the board of Northern Ontario Pipe Line Crown Corporation. H. R. Balls of the Department of Finance believes that a corporation with a minister on the board might well be-come a "corporation sole," with civil servants on the board acting in the role of advisors. [73] Still another kind of appre-hension has been expressed by a commentator who is con-cerned about preserving a measure of corporate autonomy, namely, that a minister's allegiance would be primarily to the Cabinet and not to the interests of the corporation as such. [74] Whatever the actual results of ministerial member-ship on corporate boards might be, it seems fairly certain that the experiment will have no early trial in the Canadian government.

The considerable use of deputy ministers and other senior civil servants on corporate boards inevitably raises the ques-tion of whether a distinction can logically be drawn between membership for political and administrative officials. The difference in status would seem to lessen the likelihood of domination of a board by a senior civil servant, as might be the case with a minister. A much more substantial obstacle to the use of senior civil servants as directors lies in the reconciliation of this duty with their normal departmental functions.

The question of whether the conflict of roles is too great appears to hinge largely on the seriousness with which the role-playing of all parties concerned is viewed. At first, C. D. Howe apparently felt that free discussion among members of corporate boards under his ken would be seriously hampered by the presence of his own deputy minister who, therefore, should not be a director. This rule Howe initially applied to his Crown companies [75] and, considerably earlier, to the Canadian National Railways.[76] The reversal of this rule in practice, it may be noted, was not accompanied by a public repudiation of the principle by Mr. Howe. It is logical to assume that any real conflict of roles would center on the more "discretionary" corporations, and it is to these that critics have directed their fire. J. M. Macdonnell, now a member of the Conservative Cabinet, has, on more than one occasion, taken the position that "I do not think it is fair, where decisions outside the scope of ordinary departmental decisions are to be made, to expect that civil servants are going to take a stand against their ministers. Unless they are supermen with independent incomes, how can they be expected to do it?" [77] Although not so concerned about the effects of pecuniary considerations, J. E. Hodgetts has repeatedly attacked the idea that senior departmental officers can feel a real responsibility to a corporation. To place them (or, for that matter, ministers) on a corporate board, he has written, "is akin to bringing the referee into the huddle while the signals are being called." [78] As to the specific situation of a senior civil servant, "Suppose he was outvoted in a board meeting and then had to perform the embarrassing function of fighting against 'his' corporation in front of his own political chief?" [79] In Professor Hodgetts' view, "Such administrative ambivalence is neither healthy, necessary or feasible." [80] Aside from the difficulty faced by a senior civil servant personally, Hodgetts has raised the question of whether the independence of a corporation is not seriously affected by having departmental representatives serve as directors. Although he has not committed himself as to which of the alternatives — corporate independence or dependence — is most likely to accompany a deputy minister's membership on a board, he is firm in his view that both alternatives, if they spring from this source, are undesirable.

Defense of the present arrangement revolves around the following points: first, that corporate decisions are arrived at by consensus, not status-conscious voting; second, that actual working relationships are more important than position; and, finally, that departmental views should be woven into the context of at least some corporations' decisions. As to the first point, H. R. Balls has felt that Professor Hodgetts has overstressed the importance of the divided loyalties of board members. These, he has asserted, succumb to the common desire to reach a solution to a problem. In support of this view he has cited the experience of his own deputy minister in the Department of Finance who, in his service on various boards, "did not recall a case where there had been a recorded vote. In other words, while there had been some diversity of views, these were always reconciled by discussion and agreement into a single view, that was able to be put forward as the view of the Board as a whole." [81] The second point, the influence of the informal factor of personality, is one espoused by F. A. Milligan, a student of

British and Canadian public corporations.[82] At the level of corporate-departmental dealings, he has maintained, a relatively limited number of individuals are involved, and their personal characteristics and the general atmosphere in which they meet will be more influential than the formal relations.[83] Finally, defense of the present arrangement rests perhaps mainly on the assumption, often not clearly articulated, that departmental views deserve to be given prominence in corporate counsels. In part this feeling appears to stem from a realization by all concerned of the immense value of the knowledge that an able senior civil servant can bring to bear on problems with government-wide ramifications. Interviews with corporate officials on some of the affected boards appear to confirm the genuineness of the need for including departmental representatives from the Department of Finance, in particular. Second, it can not be denied that the system of ministerial responsibility is influential in persuading ministers of the merit of the present arrangement. Thus, a former Minister of Finance, when confronted with the statement that little independence could be expected from civil servants when they served as directors, replied: "It would be hard to say where the line should be drawn as between directors of ... a public corporation ... as to what independent judgment and discretion they should exercise as directors, and the overruling powers the minister should have, who after all is the one who is responsible to parliament for the administration of the affairs of the corporation." [84] In this assertion there is at least a strong hint that coordination of corporate and ministerial action is highly desirable and that it can be achieved more smoothly by departmental representation among the directors.

CONCLUSION

In the representation given to outside forces on corporate boards, as in the organization of boards for action, variety is rampant, and generalization, in consequence, risky. For most departmental corporations or for a few other corporations whose boards are dominated by departmental representatives, the stereotype of an autonomous corporation fades rapidly, but, at the other extreme, it brightens again when such boards as those associated with the Canadian Broadcasting Corporation (pre-1958, at least) and the Canadian National Railways are examined. If a composite board is envisioned a hazy portrait at best emerges, but discernible in it are the outlines of departmental influence. Such a board might have seven to nine part-time members who engage in policy-making but leave administration to a full-time president, who also serves as chairman of the board. More likely than not, there has been an attempt to balance the board territorially and, to a lesser extent, occupationally, even without formal requirements for doing so. In considering the latter criterion, more attention has probably been given to the skills which the members bring to the board than to the aspect of representation. Additional representation through the form of an advisory committee may have been considered but probably has not been given a trial, a fact perhaps symptomatic of a relatively weak orientation toward nongovernmental influences. Some degrees of departmental influence over the board may well exist, either through formal representation or through the fact that one or more board members was associated closely in the past with the department or minister under which the corporation operates.

Accepting the variety among individual corporations, a study of direct and indirect representation on corporate boards does little to dispel a general impression, gained from material in the preceding chapter, that ministers are, with perhaps a few notable exceptions, in a strong position to put a check-rein on corporate activities and even to influence the way in which those activities are conducted in the first place. A big question remains: how does Parliament fit into the picture?

5

The Ultimate Guardian

Briefly stated, Parliament's aim with respect to public corporations must be to obtain sufficient information on their activities to enable it to discharge its obligation of holding the corporations "ultimately accountable." Given the special position of corporations — so dramatically driven home to Parliament by the early railroad debates — and the necessity to rely on ministers for much of the information, Parliament's task is a difficult one at best. When, in addition, the burden of parliamentary duties seems to increase yearly along with the size and complexity of government, the difficulties are enhanced.

In meeting the problem of corporate accountability, Parliament has not devised new techniques. Neither has it utilized the supplementary devices of consumers' councils and joint consultation between employers and employees that have been employed by the British to reinforce the total pattern of public controls. Instead Parliament has relied on the familiar techniques it has always used in holding ministries accountable: questions, debates, and committees. This chapter is concerned, then, with examining, largely through actual cases, the manner in which these traditional accountability techniques have been applied to public corporations.

THE QUESTION PERIOD

Although the question period undoubtedly deserves a Canadian writer's encomium of "one of the most formidable devices which the opposition has at its disposal," [1] its use as a technique for assuring parliamentary control over Canadian public corporations seems in practice rather spotty. As in Britain much of the difficulty can be traced to hesitation over the degree to which ministers may be questioned about the activities of corporations, but the Canadian House of Commons faces several additional obstacles. In the first place, questions have not been coupled with the British practice of giving notice of raising the matter "on the adjournment" if the questioner is dissatisfied with the answers received. Thus, a minister does not have to contend with a half-hour period at the end of each day's sitting in which the matter can be pursued at greater length. In addition, only a few Canadian corporations exist at the high level of visibility characteristic of the British nationalized industries.

An analysis of questions asked in the British House of Commons during the 1956 session is revealing as to the truth of the second point. As Table 2 indicates, only 159 questions (excluding supplementary questions) about public corporations were asked during the 152-day session.[2] An average of approximately one question a day from a House of 265 members scarcely qualifies as an indicator of strong interest in the corporations as a group. Furthermore, when the distribution of questions is analyzed it is seen that three of the corporations — the Canadian National Railways, the Canadian Broadcasting Corporation, and the Canadian Wheat Board — drew over half of the questions. Add in the Unemployment Insurance Commission and the Agricultural Prices Support Board and almost three-fourths

Table 2. Numbers of questions asked about Canadian public corporations in the House of Commons, January–August 1956.*

Name of Corporation	Minister	Questions primarily concerning —	
		Department	Corporation
1. *Departmental Corporations*			
Agricultural Prices Support Board	Agriculture	6	6
The Director, Veterans' Land Act	Veterans Affairs	2	
Dominion Coal Board	Mines and Technical Survey		1
National Gallery of Canada	Citizenship and Immigration	3	3
National Research Council	Trade and Commerce		1
Unemployment Insurance Commission	Labor	3	9
Total		14	20
2. *Agency Corporations*			
Atomic Energy of Canada Limited	Trade and Commerce		1
Crown Assets Disposal Corporation	Defence Production		2
Federal District Commission	Prime Minister		1
National Harbors Board	Transport		1
Total		0	5
3. *Proprietary Corporations*			
Canadian Broadcasting Corporation	National Revenue	3	26
Canadian National Railways	Transport	4	34
Central Mortgage and Housing Corporation	Public Works	1	7
Eldorado Mining and Refining Limited	Defence Production	1	1
St. Lawrence Seaway Authority	Transport	2	1
Trans-Canada Air Lines	Trade and Commerce	1	3
Total		12	72

* Source: tabulation by the author from *Debates*, House of Commons, Canada, for the dates mentioned.

Name of Corporation	Minister	Questions primarily concerning —	
		Department	Corporation
4. *Other*			
Bank of Canada	Finance	1	6
Canadian Wheat Board	Trade and Commerce	7	16
Industrial Development Bank	Finance		2
Northern Ontario Pipe Line Crown Corporation	Trade and Commerce	1	3
Total		9	27
Grand Total		35	124

of the questions are accounted for. Eighteen of the forty corporations (see Chapter 1 for complete list) were ignored entirely by members of the House. Granted that an analysis of questions asked in other years would bring some realignment, a spot survey indicates no major reshuffling.

Although concentration on certain corporations is understandable and perhaps can even be justified on grounds of public interest in their activities, it points up the fact that parliamentary supervision of corporations through questions is hardly systematic. It must be conceded, however, that the most cherished value of the question period in British-style parliaments has never been comprehensive coverage but the opportunity to make spot checks on the government's performance. Granting this point, the pattern of questions asked about corporations scarcely deserves this description. When it is relatively predictable that members of Parliament will be very curious about a handful of corporations and manifest little or no interest in the rest, it seems fair to say that the full potentialities of the question period as a control mechanism are not being realized.

Turning now to the caliber of the questions, it would appear that searching queries about corporate performance are rare — for reasons not unlike those in British experience.

Members of Parliament undoubtedly perform a valuable service in using the question period to pass on constituents' complaints about the relatively few corporations that deal daily with the public. In addition, how these corporations operate in his constituency is a natural object of an M.P.'s curiosity, even though the minister being questioned may strongly suspect that commercial interests hope to make profitable use of the information. Neither of these common types of questions qualifies as profound, however. It is likely that profundity is further deterred by the fact that the operations of corporations are often so technical as to make the format of the question period inapplicable for searching inquiries.

Profound or not, questions about corporate performance inevitably encounter uncertainty about their eligibility. Following upon the rule enunciated by Prime Minister Meighen in the C.N.R. debates of the twenties, ministers conventionally draw the line at answering questions about day-to-day administration (except for the departmental corporations). The perennial difficulty is that there are inevitable differences of opinion about the meaning of the term — even when it is applied to the corporation that was the reason for inventing the rule in the first place. Thus, it was contended in 1953 by John Diefenbaker, now the Conservative prime minister, that the dismissal of a C.N.R. hotel manager was not a question of internal management but one of "external interference" by ministers of the crown.[3] In response to his request for the publicizing of correspondence in the case, Diefenbaker was reminded that even Conservative ministers had consistently refused such a move. The limitations of the pioneering debates as a precedent is indicated by the fact that both sides in the 1953 discussion could cite material from them in support of their points of view. Aside from the fact that a completely satisfactory definition of day-to-day administration has never been found, the C.N.R. debates have another limitation when applied to most of the other corporations. Very few have competitors, as the C.N.R. had even when the debates were staged, and hence lack this powerful reason for maintaining secrecy about the conduct of their affairs. Yet, in 1953 the Liberal Minister of Resources and Development cited the C.N.R. debates in support of his refusal to furnish information about salaries paid to top officials of the Central Mortgage and Housing Corporation, a noncompeting corporation. True, the Minister's position — that these debates established "the principle governing the relationship between crown corporations and parliament" [4] — probably is more widely accepted than a view that restricts the precedent to corporations with competitors. As the precedent was shaped under competitive conditions, however, members of Parliament who seek information are sometimes reluctant, as some were in this case, to accept a broader application of the rule against disclosing information about day-to-day administration.

The limits of the question hour as an information-gathering device are indicated by the frequency with which questioners are referred to other media, notably committee hearings. In the first example cited in the preceding paragraph, for instance, Mr. Diefenbaker was encouraged to attend the appropriate committee hearing and learn from railway officials themselves the answers to his queries. A similar suggestion was made to J. M. Macdonnell, then the opposition's financial critic, when he asked the Minister of Finance about the significance of a rise in the Bank of Canada's interest rate.[5] In reply Macdonnell asked whether the opportunity to query the governor of the bank in committee hearings later should preclude an answer from the minister. The Minister stated that no one "would seriously

expect me to make a reasoned statement about monetary
policy on the orders of the day," and suggested that if further discussion of the interest rate were desired after the
governor's appearance before the Banking and Commerce
Committee, time would be provided for debate in the
House.[6]

The House's rule that ministers may refuse to answer a
question, may refuse to give a reason for the refusal, and
may not be subjected to debate on their stand, occasionally
serves as a last-ditch stand for ministers questioned about
the activities of corporations under their supervision. Asked
why the Canadian Broadcasting Corporation had dropped
its review of a book about the late Mackenzie King, the Minister of National Revenue gave the reason furnished him by
the corporation.[7] Pressed further some days later, the Minister stated that "the corporation advises" that it carries
full responsibility for programming.[8] Asked finally whether
the person in the C.B.C. who made the decision would be
identified, the Minister, after a lapse of a week during
which he had promised to consult corporation officials,
would not go beyond his previous answer. Opposition protests were cut short by the Speaker, who quoted the rule
summarized above.[9] Again, when the opposition has been
reluctant to accept the suggestion that other media be used
to obtain an answer to a question, the rule has served the
government well. In replying to a request for information
about the C.N.R.'s coal purchases for specified routes and
periods of time, the Minister of Transport stated that, in the
railway's opinion, collecting the information would be costly
and time-consuming and would only inspire similar requests.[10] Faced with insistence upon an answer, the Minister reminded the House that "the practice of the Canadian
National Railways, one that has been accepted in the house
for years, is that if information of this nature is required

it may be asked at a sitting of the committee on railways and shipping." [11] The opposition leader saw in this statement a suggestion that the question was not improper and pressed the government for an immediate answer. Eventually the Speaker ended the controversy by citing the Minister's right to decline to answer.

Corporations differ considerably, depending upon the degree of independence from the minister to whom they report, in the amount of discretion they have in answering questions. As the examples above suggest, the Canadian National Railways and the Canadian Broadcasting Corporation are two corporations that approach autonomy in this respect. It is doubtful, however, whether a corporation can follow a restrictive policy about furnishing information without incurring risks in Parliament. For example, in the last-mentioned case above, the Prime Minister suggested that although "I do not know whether the house can make an order that would be effective on the Canadian National Railways that they supply that information at this time," the question might stand while the C.N.R. digested the fact that the opposition was not satisfied with the answer given. [12]

DEBATES

Aside from the question period, opportunities for discussing public corporations on the floor of the House may arise in two general ways, namely, when the subject matter for debate is wide open under House rules and when some aspect of corporate affairs is the order of business. In the first category are the lengthy debates on the Speech from the Throne and the budget, as well as debates on motions to adjourn the House to discuss "a definite matter of urgent public importance" or to go into Committee of Supply or Committee of Ways and Means. In the second category are debates on legislation amending statutes under which corporations operate, on establishing committees to review their activities, and on supplying funds to them.

The debates on the Speech from the Throne and the budget, sometimes referred to as the two main "sporting events" of the season for members of the House, are long on opportunities to mention corporations but short on opportunities to discuss them thoroughly in the give-and-take of debate. Since virtually any topic can be mentioned in his allotted forty minutes, it is customary for a member to parade oratorically through the field of public issues with a minimum of regard for the comments of previous speakers and with a somewhat unfortunate effect on the attention of his audience, especially since this process is repeated by his colleagues over a period of several weeks. The broad latitude given to speakers in these two debates does serve the purpose of permitting mention of grievances and undoubtedly acts as a kind of safety valve for the average member of the House. The prominence of public corporations in these discussions is indicated by the fact that in 1956 seven corporations or activities with which corporations were concerned were mentioned in the brief Speech from the Throne.[13] The ten solid days of debate that followed saw frequent mention of other corporations,[14] as well as numerous references to those mentioned in the Speech. Although the budget debate of 1956 did not cover as many corporations, the pattern was much the same.

Because their purpose is more limited, better coordinated discussions are likely to emerge from motions to adjourn the House for the purpose of discussing a definite matter of urgent public importance or to go into Committee of Supply or Committee of Ways and Means. The restrictions on the former device, however, appear to be sufficiently formidable to prevent its widespread use. The Speaker has the power to disallow the motion and customarily interprets the rules about "urgency" and permissible topics strictly. A perusal of the 1956 *Debates* indicates that only five motions to adjourn the House for the purpose of discussing a definite matter of urgent public importance were made. Of these, none dealt directly with public corporations and all were declared out of order by the Speaker. A motion for the House to go into Committee of Supply or Committee of Ways and Means is the occasion for members to air grievances on almost any subject.[15] Such a motion is made by a minister, who may elect to open the discussion himself, although he usually does not. Of the six debates on motions to go into Committee of Supply recorded in the 1956 *Debates*, two involved discussion of public corporations. On February 7, during the first of the six debates, a member of the opposition raised questions about the cancellation of a Canadian Broadcasting Corporation program and engaged in a controversy with members of the Cabinet about the question of interference with the C.B.C. (pp. 945–948). On March 12 the basic act under which the former Agricultural Prices Support Board operated came in for criticism because of "glaring inconsistencies in its administration" (p. 2021). On the following day, in a continuation of debate under the same motion, an opposition member criticized "dictatorship in the unemployment insurance commission" (p. 2113). Of the three instances, only the second-named was sufficiently extensive to deserve the title of "debate," and it may be noted that the precise point mentioned occupied only a minor place in a lengthy discussion of the government's agricultural policy. A motion to go into Committee of Ways and Means was employed only once — to launch a discussion of international affairs (pp. 709 ff.).

As might be expected, the heart of parliamentary discussion of public corporations is found, not in the more general types of debates mentioned above, but when a specific aspect of corporate affairs is the order of business, the second broad category mentioned at the beginning of this section. Debates on bills amending legislation under which corporations operate will be considered first. It is apparent that such debates do afford the opportunity for comments upon the record of affected corporations, judging by the 1956 *Debates.* For example, when the government moved that the House go into committee to consider a resolution dealing with a housing measure, an opposition speaker seized the occasion to cite examples of ways in which "the corporation is becoming increasingly bureaucratic in its attitude and behavior" (pp. 3171 ff.). An examination of the other eight debates in this category, however, indicates that the House usually was not this aggressive about discussing corporate administration. Debate on a bill amending the Industrial Development Bank Act, for instance, included discussion of the proper role of the bank (pp. 3650–58, 3675–78) but no comments on its administration of existing statutes.

Motions for establishing committees to review the operations of specific public corporations provide a second, and probably more important, occasion for discussion of corporate operations. True, relatively few corporations are involved because Parliament's tendency is to take this step only for the more prominent or the more controversial corporations. Given this limitation, however, the situation is ready-made for pointed discussion of issues involving these particular corporations, and it is apparent from the debates that participants are well primed. It would also appear that the more frequently a committee is set up to review the operations of the corporation the more informed and disciplined is the discussion on the floor. The debates on setting up committees to examine the Canadian National Railways and affiliated corporations or the Canadian Broadcasting

Corporation, for instance, tend to march in almost predictable fashion through the gamut of issues made familiar by repetition through the years. In the former case, this means discussion of such issues as the necessity for the C.N.R. to show a profit, the kind of equipment used, the level of pensions for retired employees, and the question of competition for Trans-Canada Air Lines, a subsidiary of the railroad. As to the C.B.C., questions are likely to be raised on the subject of making one agency both operator and regulator (before 1958), the choice of programs, and the method of financing the corporation. Even for those corporations whose operations are not so regularly reviewed, such as the Federal District Commission, it is apparent that members of the House view the debate on the motion to establish a committee as a suitable occasion for airing questions about the corporation that have come to their attention.

Debates on furnishing funds to corporations, the final occasion for discussion of corporations on the floor of the House, resemble the type just discussed in certain important ways. Again, not all corporations (that is, those which do not require parliamentary appropriations) are, or at least need be, included. It will be remembered that departmental corporations "must look to Parliament for annual appropriations," agency corporations have a "normal dependence on Parliamentary appropriations for deficit financing," and proprietary corporations "are ordinarily required to pay their own way." [16] A further point of similarity is the broad range of discussion about certain corporations. Traditionally, discussion of the "estimates" is a zealously guarded right of Parliament, a time when the private member is thought to come into his own. The scope of the discussion is influenced by the wording of the item under discussion. For example, on the following item pertaining to the National Gallery of Canada, a departmental corporation under the Minister of Citizenship and Immigration, it was required that discussion follow closely the terms of reference: "548. Payment to the national gallery purchase account for the purpose of acquiring works of art in conformity with section 8 of the National Gallery Act — further amount required, $885,000." [17] When, however, such a general item as "Departmental Administration" is up for discussion, the debate may range far and wide over departmental affairs, including even the operations of corporations for which no specific appropriations are being made. Under this item in 1956, for instance, the Minister of Defence Production referred to two agency corporations, the Canadian Commercial Corporation and Crown Assets Disposal Corporation which "require no appropriation since they are financed by means of a surcharge on the volume of business handled," [18] and subsequent discussion included questions on the activities of these corporations. [19]

Paradoxically enough, the two corporations that in 1956 received the most generous quota of discussion were two proprietary corporations, part of a group normally expected to conduct their operations without appropriations. Consistent with the tendency observed in types of debates reviewed earlier, the Canadian Broadcasting Corporation and the Canadian National Railways (together with its subsidiary, Trans-Canada Air Lines) were discussed in considerable detail in Committee of Supply. Again, certain favorite issues involving these corporations dominated the discussion. Aside from absorption in such issues as "monopoly," the House was stimulated to spend approximately seven hours on the C.B.C. by the fact that 1956 marked the automatic termination of a system, set up by statute in 1951, whereby an annual grant was made to the corporation without subjecting it to the normal estimates procedure. [20] Consideration of Department of Transport estimates produced discussion of the C.N.R. under three items, some bearing only a remote relationship to the railroad.[21] In similar fashion, Trans-Canada Air Lines was discussed under three items in the departmental estimates.[22] The attention given these two corporations becomes even more impressive considering the fact that their affairs customarily are thoroughly aired in the hearings held by the Sessional Committee on Railways and Shipping Owned, Operated and Controlled by the Government. In addition, both corporations come in for further discussion in the House when the annual Canadian National Railways Financing and Guarantee Act is before the House in bill form.[23]

Broad as is the scope of discussion on certain items in the estimates, a considerable sense of frustration about the efficacy of the procedure is apparently felt in the House, particularly when corporations are involved. An illustration of this feeling is provided by an incident in 1953 involving the National Film Board (not a public corporation but a somewhat analogous body). George A. Drew, then leader of the Conservatives, objected in the following terms to the absence of parliamentary influence in the decision to transfer board headquarters from Ottawa to Montreal:

I conceded without any reservation that all members of Parliament, in varying degrees, must accept some responsibility for a system which appears to result in decisions through the acceptance of items in the estimates which constitute, in fact, the only authority for proceeding with a great number of these activities.

. . . there is no course open to the opposition to prevent these things happening, except to talk indefinitely on a single item. There is no recorded vote in the ordinary way on division . . .

. . . there is no opportunity for orderly debate, for examination of any records or for an understanding of what the policy of the government really is.[24]

Despite complaints of the type noted, there is often a kind

of wistful yearning that more corporations be subjected to the procedure. Typical is the following statement, made in anticipation of increased control through the proposed Financial Administration Act:

As you know, in the past these propriety [sic] corporations did not need to report to parliament. Just as long as they were not running in the hole they could go on for years and years without ever coming under parliamentary scrutiny . . . It has been only those corporations that do not pile up a surplus but must come back to parliament each year to get either grants or loans or money to make up their deficits that have been subject to annual parliamentary scrutiny. I think most hon. members would like to have a good look at operations of the successful corporations as well as at the unsuccessful corporations . . .[25]

In looking at the whole range of debates on corporations in the House the observer is struck by the absence of the type which has been characterized in Great Britain as "the best opportunity of reviewing the work of the Boards [of the nationalized industries]," namely, debates on the annual reports.[26] In the Canadian House the tabling of an annual report is quite unobtrusive, being accompanied at most with a brief comment by a minister and, in cases where a pertinent committee is sitting, a motion to refer the report to the committee.[27] It would be unfair, however, to say that this is the only mention of annual reports in the House. In connection with debates on the estimates, ministers sometimes make a point of summarizing the contents of an annual report and directly or indirectly invite discussion of the contents. In 1956, for example, the Minister of National Revenue, after summarizing the annual report of the Canadian Broadcasting Corporation, commented that he hoped this action would "make a basis for discussion."[28] In the debate that followed and in other debates on estimates of the Department of Transport and the Department of Defence

Production, with which are connected numerous corporations, a number of references were made to the contents of annual reports.[29] In comparing Canadian practice with the British it must also be noted that the former probably allows fuller examination in committees of such annual reports as are referred. Preliminary committee examination would seem to assure a higher quality of debate in the House. It must be said, however, that the House does not discuss the reports of its committees but instead permits them to be tabled without comment,[30] or agrees without debate to a motion to concur in the report.[31] In so doing the House would seem to be missing a fine opportunity for informed debate on the more prominent public corporations.

PARLIAMENTARY COMMITTEES

In attacking the problem of supervising corporate activities through committees, the Canadian House of Commons has, apparently without much planning, followed two main approaches. First, it has made some attempt to adapt an old instrument of accountability, the Committee on Public Accounts, to the purpose of obtaining general financial supervision of corporations. Secondly, it has made rather sporadic, but increasing, use of standing or select committees whose task it is to examine the activities of certain corporations. The salient details of these approaches are considered in the ensuing pages.

The Committee on Public Accounts, which, as its name suggests, has the function of examining the *Public Accounts of Canada*, dates back to the first meeting of the Canadian Parliament after federation. Lacking many of the virtues of the British committee for which it was named, the Canadian Committee has often been criticized for "its large size, its composition, its partisan attitude, and the infrequency of its meetings." [32] Of the committee's fifty members in 1956, thirty-two, including the chairman and vice-chairman, were members of the party in power. According to a statement of the committee chairman in 1956, the committee "has assembled six times in twenty-one years." [33] Like most other parliamentary committees, it meets only at the request of a member of the committee, although it has been appointed regularly and the *Public Accounts* and the auditor general's *Report* have usually been referred to it. Despite this record, the committee is not without influence because its reports are usually given a great deal of publicity, its comments and criticisms are said to be carefully noted by departments, and the mere possibility of investigation of any expenditure probably has a salutary influence on the executive branch.[34]

Whatever the shortcomings of the Public Accounts Committee, it has not been unaware of the special problem posed by public corporations. Its concern for corporate accountability was summed up in recommendations made to the House in 1951 that "the annual reports of all Crown Corporations be published together in one section of the Public Accounts" and that "the annual report of every Crown Corporation should be referred for study to a select committee of the House." [35] The first recommendation was promptly adopted by the House and by the minister of finance, who annually presents the *Public Accounts of Canada* to the governor general. Since 1952 the second volume of this publication has presented the financial statements of all agency and proprietary corporations and the auditors' reports on those statements. Previously, corporate statements had been scattered throughout the *Public Accounts,* and statements of those corporations whose accounts were audited by private auditors were left out. Inclusion of the entire range of financial statements and reports means that, unlike British practice, no special reference is required in order to discuss them in the Public Accounts Committee.

Simplification of the committee's power to examine the financial records of corporations seems not to have produced much more thorough examinations so far. Corporate representatives and ministers to whom corporations report are not ordinarily called for questioning. In the time at the committee's disposal — many accounts other than corporations' must, of course, be examined — testimony is usually limited to the auditor general and witnesses from the Department of Finance. It should be noted, however, that the auditor general is of much greater aid to the committee than is the case in Great Britain where special commercial auditors audit the accounts of the nationalized industries. In Canada the auditor general at present audits the accounts of all but seven public corporations.[36] When the committee proceeds through the Crown corporation section of the *Report of the Auditor General to the House of Commons* paragraph by paragraph, members have an opportunity to ask him questions about each agency and proprietary corporation (departmental corporations being lumped with departments). In 1956 roughly two hours were spent in questioning the auditor general on the section of his *Report* dealing with Crown corporations, and two officials of the Department of Finance were questioned for an additional hour and a quarter. In this amount of time, which is not far from typical, it is hardly possible to delve very deeply into the financial record of individual corporations. The paragraphs in the *Report* which naturally draw the most attention are those containing criticisms or suggestions. In 1956, for example, the committee discussed the auditor general's criticism of the "inconsistency in practice" with regard to fire insurance in the various corporations.[37] At the auditor general's suggestion, the deputy minister of finance was asked about the matter when he appeared before the committee, and he defended the lack of uniformity principally "because you have not got uniform conditions." [38] The matter was not pressed further.

Several points can be made in defense of the Public Accounts Committee's relatively mild review of the financial accounts of public corporations. The committee obviously has great confidence in the ability of the auditor general to turn up questionable financial practices. Also, committee members display a commendable diffidence in admitting that, as presently constituted and operated, their committee may not be the best one to deal with certain corporations' financial reports and in urging reference of these reports to select committees.[39] Enthusiasm of committee members may be further blunted by the realization that public accounts are "ancient history" and that "we can only examine [corporate] expenditures to the extent that they are covered in public accounts." [40] Finally, it is conceivable, as some British politicians and administrators have warned, that a very active role by a public accounts committee might drastically upset a system of managerial autonomy for corporations.[41]

Criticisms of the committee's procedure for scrutinizing the public accounts of corporations inevitably hearken back to the general criticisms of the committee recounted earlier. Even if a decisive change, involving a shift to a small, able group headed by a chairman from the opposition may not be politically feasible, definite improvements over the present haphazard arrangement could be obtained without much difficulty. If the committee held sessions each year an improvement in expertise might be expected. In addition, such a plan would allow the committee to single out several corporations at random each year for a more detailed review than is now possible. Finally, the use of subcommittees to make detailed reviews — a plan discussed by the committee itself in 1950 [42] — might be given a trial.

Probably the strongest argument against strengthening the Public Accounts Committee is the existence of standing or select committees which now review the financial activities of certain public corporations in some detail. In the opinion of some observers the number and variety of these committees is sufficient to permit an extension of this procedure to all public corporations. The Public Accounts Committee itself, as we have seen, has endorsed this idea.

Actually, there is at present only one House committee which *regularly* considers the annual reports of public corporations, although several other committees follow this procedure with varying degrees of regularity. The Sessional Committee on Railways and Shipping Owned, Operated and Controlled by the Government annually reviews the reports and budgets of the Canadian National Railways, Trans-Canada Air Lines, and Canadian National (West Indies) Steamships Limited, as well as the auditors' reports on these corporations. With less regularity the following committees have discussed the reports of the corporations listed in parentheses: Special Committee on Broadcasting (Canadian Broadcasting Corporation); Standing Committee on Agriculture and Colonization (Canadian Wheat Board); Standing Committee on Banking and Commerce (Bank of Canada, Industrial Development Bank, and Central Mortgage and Housing Corporation). Review of reports at more infrequent intervals is provided in a few cases where it is thought desirable to bring Parliament abreast of developments in certain fields. Thus, special committees were set up in 1949, 1952–53, and 1956 to review developments in the growing group of public corporations directly or indirectly related to the atomic energy program (at present the National Research Council, Atomic Energy Control Board, Atomic Energy of Canada Limited, Eldorado Mining and Refining Limited, Eldorado Aviation Limited, and Northern Transportation Limited).[43]

Recognizing the risks of generalization in this instance, impressions about the character of committee review will, nevertheless, be catalogued. The usual procedure is to call corporate officials and to proceed through the annual report of a corporation (and perhaps the budget and auditor's report as well) heading by heading, the pace being governed by the number and intricacy of the questions directed at the corporate officials who testify.[44] As might be expected, the committees which meet with the greatest regularity appear to have achieved the greatest efficiency in this process, seemingly a strong argument for extending the principle of regular supervision of public corporations by a series of committees dealing with various governmental fields.

One is tempted at first glance to conclude that regularity of meeting is the criterion for the frequency of politically motivated questions, and that this argues against regularity. A more accurate statement is that the degree of controversy surrounding a corporation is the actual criterion. The same committee, for example, deals with both the Canadian National Railways and the Trans-Canada Air Lines, but the questions asked about the latter corporation in recent years reflect its deeper involvement in a major policy question of the day, namely, whether public corporations should have competition from private sources. For the same reason, the proceedings of the committee which supervises the Canadian Broadcasting Corporation (but meets somewhat less regularly than the Railways Committee) probably contain a higher proportion of questions based upon policy stands of the political parties than is found in the proceedings of any other committee. Certain aspects of banking, credit, and housing policy also seem to draw politically motivated questions in the Standing Committee on Banking and Commerce. When it comes to the Special Committee on Research, which meets every third year or so to review rapidly unfolding developments in a relatively technical and fluid field, straight requests for information are notably prevalent.

The behavior charted above is, of course, a normal phenomenon, one not necessarily to be deplored. Questions inspired by the questioner's position on controversial policy matters not only are inevitable but may have the virtue — when considered as a whole — of intensifying the alertness of the committees as instruments of accountability. In the abstract, impartial, detached questioning might be longed for, but it is unrealistic to expect it so long as individual corporations remain controversial.

From the record it does not appear that corporate officials are hounded unfairly by the type of questioning they undergo. Interrogation of officials is under two quite different types of restrictions, namely, a committee's terms of reference and the existence of an area of discretion reserved to management. If opposition members seek to bring a discussion of major policy questions into a review of the reports of corporations, the watchful majority on the committee will in all probability vote down the motion. This, for instance, was the fate in 1956 of a Conservative motion to call witnesses for private air lines before the Railways and Shipping Committee to testify on future prospects for air traffic.[45] The majority interpreted this proposal as an attempt to debate the government policy of preserving a government monopoly on transcontinental air service and cited the terms of the committee's assigned duty to "consider the accounts and estimates and bills relating thereto."[46] A second escape route for hard-pressed corporate officials is by way of the claim of managerial discretion. When, for example, opposition members of the Railways and Shipping Committee pressed Donald Gordon, the president of the Canadian National Railways, for reasons why a Canadian advertising agency had been replaced by an American one for the United States advertising area, they were told only that it was "a matter of policy on our part." [47] For the same reason, an opposition motion to call and question witnesses from the Canadian aircraft industry regarding the types of planes purchased by Trans-Canada Air Lines was defeated. [48]

From the standpoint of corporate officials, supervision by a parliamentary committee might be viewed at times either as a partial restriction on freedom of action or as affording a forum for defense against unfriendly forces. Corporations much in the public eye but dependent on Parliament for financial aid, such as the Canadian National Railways and the Canadian Broadcasting Corporation, probably feel the effects of committee supervision most heavily. For example, after the president of the railways, in testifying before the Sessional Committee on Railways and Shipping, had strongly defended the right of management to "exercise its judgment in the interests of the property it is managing," the following exchange took place.

Mr. FULTON: In this respect do you feel you have any greater or lesser freedom of action to exercise judgment than would the board of directors of an ordinary commercial company?

Mr. GORDON: Very much less discretion, I think, for the reason that we always have very much in mind that when we accept the responsibility we are obliged to account for everything that we do right here, and we are dealing with the sort of thing that can come up in the House of Commons at any time. Therefore we tend to hold our discretion just to those things which can be proved beyond peradventure . . . If we were more flexible we could do more intelligent planning and perhaps do a better job — it is hard to say.

Mr. CHURCHILL: Mr. Chairman, I do not quite see that

there is any lack of flexibility. Is there any instance where decisions have had to be changed or refused on a review such as this?

Mr. GORDON: Never, because we have always been careful to so anticipate your decision that it cannot be refused. But I say we have to exercise our judgment in the light of that . . .[49]

When corporate officials are not yearning for the freedom of private business, however, they may view the role of parliamentary committees somewhat differently. For example, on the basis of his "close contact with the directors and managers of a good many of these Crown companies," the auditor general went so far as to state to the Public Accounts Committee that these officials "feel that they have a good story to tell and that they would like to tell that story. Furthermore, they feel that there is some suspicion as to the way Crown corporations are operated and they would like to clear themselves of that, to tell their little problems and to tell of their successes, and usually they feel that it would be healthier to have their story told in public."[50] A longing to tell their story publicly is characteristic chiefly of the corporate officials who rarely get a chance to do so before a committee, but even the closely supervised Canadian Broadcasting Corporation has felt the benefits of the practice, according to one observer's analysis of the operations of the Special Committee on Broadcasting: "It is the one forum available to officials of the Corporation for the defence of their actions against the criticisms of such organized groups as the Canadian Association of Broadcasters. In addition, the committee has eased the political pressure on the Corporation in helping it to decide policy on controversial issues, or at least backing up decisions already taken by the Corporation."[51] Between the two corporate views about committee supervision illustrated above there may be another — summed up by the philosophy of "let sleeping dogs lie." Even in the disciplined parliamentary form of government there can be uncertainty about what will emerge once legislators begin probing.

To summarize, the question of the adequacy of parliamentary committees as instruments of accountability breaks down into several components. The first is the matter of coverage. Some public corporations are much more familiar to the average M.P. than others, and these come under relatively close and steady surveillance. The familiarity of committee members with such corporations as the Canadian National Railways, Trans-Canada Air Lines, and the Canadian Broadcasting Corporation is reflected in the frequency with which reference is made in the hearings to personal experiences with them. Generally speaking, these corporations are the most important ones in the country and deserve the most attention. It is questionable, however, whether the low level of visibility of the remainder of the corporations justifies the committees and Parliament itself in ignoring them almost completely. Members of Parliament may be justified in complaining that they are asked to approve corporate activities without adequate review, but it must be noted that they have not taken full advantage of such devices as are available to them. The Public Accounts Committee has for long had a practice whereby corporate officials can be called for questioning at the request of any member,[52] but the requests have apparently not been forthcoming. The government in its turn, could facilitate the review of corporation reports by providing for their automatic reference to standing committees, as some M.P.s have suggested from time to time.[53]

If the range of review by parliamentary committees leaves something to be desired, what of the caliber of review now accorded the activities of certain prominent corporations? Certainly the heads of these corporations must submit to exhaustive questioning about their activities. The generally

high caliber of these officials is evidenced by their knowl-
edgeability about many aspects of corporate affairs, by the
plaudits which they often receive from the committee, and
by the respect they appear to have earned throughout the
country. A perusal of committee hearings indicates wide
agreement on the efficiency with which such veteran officials as Donald Gordon of the Canadian National Railways,
James E. Coyne of the Bank of Canada, and A. Davidson
Dunton of the (pre-1958) Canadian Broadcasting Corporation have operated their respective corporations.

Some dissatisfaction with the caliber of review revolves
about the feeling of opposition members of committees that
more information than is now provided is necessary in order
to judge the performance of a public corporation that has
private counterparts. Frequently, when officials of T.C.A.,
C.N.R., and C.B.C. give performance data they are asked
about similar figures for private companies in Canada and
the United States. These are generally supplied to the best
of the officials' abilities and, if favorable to the public corporation, draw expressions of approval. Otherwise, explana-
tions are requested. Proposals for questioning representatives of private industry by way of obtaining more data have
run into two kinds of roadblocks in the Railways and Shipping Committee. The majority has pointed out, first, that
private industry dare not publicize details of its operations
when there are indications that the government-owned railroad and airline would be delighted to have such information.[54] Secondly, when the majority of the committee has
suspected that testimony from private industry was actually
being sought in order to aid the opposition in challenging
government policy, the request has been voted down. In the
Special Committee on Broadcasting — which also deals
with a segment of the economy in which there is both
public and private enterprise — representatives of private

industry have customarily been called to testify and to answer questions dealing with statements made by officials of the Canadian Broadcasting Corporation. Representatives of labor and other groups have also appeared. The terms of reference of this committee have customarily been broader than those of the Railways Committee, however. They include not only the duty to examine the annual report but also "to review the policies and aims of the Corporation and its regulations, revenues, expenditures and development." [55] The broader mandate probably can be traced in part to the existence of regulatory powers for the C.B.C. and the fact that the committee does not meet every year. The result of the appearance of numerous private groups is a thorough airing of the operations of the C.B.C. and the general outlines of government policy. With the help of ammunition gathered in the 1955 hearings, the opposition sought unsuccessfully to include in the committee's final report motions expressing strong disapproval of the Canadian Broadcasting Corporation's possession of regulatory powers, financial arrangements, and "monopoly." [56]

In conclusion, parliamentary committees are an important link in the chain of accountability for Canadian Crown corporations, but it is apparent that the link is not uniformly strong and has been forged more by accident than design. In theory the Public Accounts Committee represents the closest approach to systematic, comprehensive review, but the committee's shortcomings have been noted. The committee's own contribution to system — the suggestion that all annual corporate reports be referred to appropriate standing committees — is less likely of adoption than the continued gradual evolution of the standing committee system as the pace of events seems to demand. For example, the increasing complexity of the atomic energy field may bring annual committee review to the various corporations associated with it more quickly than is now anticipated.

CONCLUSION

Parliament's reliance on familiar techniques in order to hold corporations "ultimately accountable" puts great emphasis upon maximum use of those techniques. The data in this chapter appear to indicate that Parliament has not entirely met this test. The question period, in particular, fails tests of comprehensiveness and profundity and is subject to difficulties about the eligibility of questions because of the ambiguous position of public corporations. On balance it must be said, however, that these limitations are not peculiar to Canada and that there are undoubted merits in the question period. Debates, the second technique, offer numerous opportunities of varying degrees of effectiveness for discussing public corporations. In the category of wide-open debates, motions to go into Committee of Supply or of Ways and Means appear to furnish the best occasions for discussion of specific grievances about corporations, although in 1956, for example, such motions were used for this purpose only a few times. Better coordinated discussions are likely to emerge from the second category of debates, those dealing specifically with some aspect of corporate affairs. In this category debates on bills amending corporate statutes can be penetrating but are, by their own terms, limited in coverage. Much the same statement can be made about debates on motions to set up committees to review the activities of one or more corporations, especially since relatively few corporations get this kind of scrutiny by standing or select committees. Debates on proposed government expenditures offer an opportunity to mention every corporation because under the item of "departmental administration" even those corporations for which expenditures are not listed can be discussed. Actually, the discussion here, as in most other debates, is skewed heavily toward those few corporations in which Parliament has a great interest, whereas other corporations are slighted. Of the three accountability techniques employed by Parliament, the use of committees appears to offer the greatest promise in helping Parliament to give systematic attention to corporations. So far, however, the Standing Committee on Public Accounts seems to have taken little advantage of the fact that it now receives the financial records of all corporations. The committee itself apparently considers that only standing or select committees are in a position to make thorough investigations of corporate activities. Although Parliament has made increasing use of such committees, it would take many years at the present rate before complete coverage were obtained, and various factors militate against its happening. Suggestions for improvements in the use of Parliament's accountability techniques will be considered in the concluding chapter.

6

Public Ownership and Accountability

Canadian public corporations, like those of numerous other countries, lack homogeneity and defy easy classification. In this study the fact of incorporation has been used as the simplest and most obvious criterion for definition of the over-all category, but it is apparent that even this elementary fact may not be disclosed by the title of some corporations. Here again Canada is not unique. So frustrating has been the effort at description that John Thurston in writing about "government proprietary corporations in the English-speaking countries" some years ago concluded that even the use of the word corporation was undeserved because "the essential idea of a corporation is that of a group of natural persons united in the desire to pursue certain purposes and achieve certain ends.... Rather, what we have is a public agency created by the legislature, forming a part of the government, and managed by persons who are servants of the state."[1] Whatever may be the merits of using the term "corporation" for these government bodies, Thurston's comment points up the fact that government corporations cannot be viewed as entities isolated from the remainder of the government.

One outstanding difficulty of classification is that functional characteristics do not necessarily correspond with

131

constitutional characteristics, as D. N. Chester has pointed out.[2] Granted the difficulty, the attempt made in the Canadian Financial Administration Act to classify "Crown corporations" according to the degree of financial independence as well as the general nature of their activity has come off rather well. Even so, it has left a residue of a half-dozen corporations which, for one reason or another, have not been classed as departmental, agency, or proprietary corporations.

As in most countries, Canadian public corporations have been strongly — though certainly not exclusively — identified with the furnishing of economic services. Here, as elsewhere, the pattern of national development has influenced the pattern of corporate development. The Canadian scene is characterized by the active and varied use of corporations, by few theoretical underpinnings for the employment of the corporate form, and, finally, by the prominence of pragmatic considerations in the context of a national drive for economic and cultural self-sufficiency. Yet, despite the willingness to create public corporations whenever the nation's progress seems to demand it, corporations that dispense commercial goods and services to the public are less numerous and, on the whole, less prominent than in Britain, with its huge nationalized industries. This fact is largely explained by the absence of an ideological drive for nationalization and a basic assumption that private enterprise is preferable if it measures up to the task. "Measuring up" is not necessarily restricted to economic criteria, however. The cultural importance of wireless communications media, for example, has resulted in the primacy of a government corporation in that field, without much attention to the economic costs. Even where economics is more influential, as in transcontinental transportation, nationalistic considerations have affected the role assigned to public corporations.

Such considerations are, of course, considerably more influential in national defense, an area which has spawned the largest number of corporations in the years since the beginning of World War II.

In speculating about future attitudes toward government corporations in Canada, it is pertinent to note the existence of two rather contradictory trends. The first is the growing strength of the private enterprise sector of the economy, a trend aided by the policies of the Conservative government that came to power in 1957 and was greatly strengthened by its smashing victory at the polls in 1958. Both in radio-television and in aviation the Diefenbaker government has indicated that it will take steps intended to give more encouragement to private efforts to develop these fields. At the same time, there are no signs that government corporations in these fields will be eliminated or even have their operations seriously curtailed by these measures. The Conservatives' own zeal to preserve Canadian identity and culture should prevent the granting of such sweeping concessions to private broadcasters as to displace the Canadian Broadcasting Corporation from its position of cultural leadership. In aviation the announced terms for broader competition give to Trans-Canada Air Lines an opportunity to invade private areas, just as its own domain is no longer to be inviolable. In a sense the Conservatives seem to be applying to wireless communications and aviation the policy originally applied to transcontinental railroads, namely, that the public interest is best protected through competition. In certain fields now dominated by government corporations but having potential exploitation value for private industry — such as atomic energy — it may be anticipated that pressures for a change in governmental policy will build up during the coming years. A second trend pertaining to government corporations has — at least until the recent Conservative victories at the polls —seemed to favor the continued and expanded use of these instruments. This is the constantly expanding role assigned to government, first, in assuring defense of the country in an age of missiles and atomic weapons, and, second, in following its traditional role of pioneering in national economic development. So challenging are the remaining economic frontiers and so urgent is the need for their quick development that government could not evade its responsibilities if it wished to do so. The St. Lawrence Seaway Authority, Northern Ontario Pipe Line Crown Corporation, Northern Canada Power Commission, and Northern Transportation Company Limited are recent examples of the use of corporations for developmental tasks. Although the Diefenbaker government has placed great stress on developing the great Canadian northland, it is less certain that the Conservatives have quite the same faith as their predecessors in the use of corporations for this or other purposes. Judging by their attitude when they were in opposition and during the first year or so after taking over the reins of government, they will be inclined to explore the capabilities of private enterprise more thoroughly than the Liberals, and, if government action still seems called for, will not resort so automatically to the corporate device. To the extent that the two trends reviewed above are still contradictory, it is likely that they can exist side by side without producing a kind of corporate schizophrenia because they are not in direct conflict (except potentially in the atomic energy area). When the economic frontiers have all been conquered — a condition not likely to be reached soon — the situation may be quite different. Then, assuming that private enterprise has continued its vigorous growth, the clamor for government to yield its domain may be heard on a wide front. The periodic drive conducted by American conservatives to "get the government out of business" may furnish a guide to eventual Canadian experience — at least for those corporations that find themselves in some form of competition with business.

The generalizations made above about the future of Canadian public corporations have little relevance to existing corporations that perform management or research functions. Their place seems assured, in any event, since their functions are so vital to governmental, and even national, purposes. Aside from this point, most of them fall into the category of "departmental corporations" that perform what the Financial Administration Act calls "administrative, supervisory, or regulatory services of a governmental nature." Fluctuations in sentiment about whether private or public enterprise should perform a function have little effect on corporations performing tasks much like those of government bureaus. Clothing them in the corporate mantle does raise a question about an indiscriminate resort to public corporations. Undoubtedly, there is merit in the argument sometimes made that the process of litigation is simplified through incorporation. Yet, the fact that at least four departmental corporations [3] are exempted by their statutes from the provisions of the Civil Service Act creates the suspicion that incorporation may have been a way of avoiding personnel controls. Though there is a legitimate argument for permitting certain public corporations to have their own personnel system, it is difficult to justify the arrangement in at least two of these cases.

The variety in Canadian public corporations makes it difficult to give categorical answers to traditional questions about accountability. Is corporate accountability adequate for the purposes of democratic government and, more particularly, for the purposes of a parliamentary system on the British model? Does the system of accountability interfere unduly with the operational freedom of corporations?

The various British nationalized industries have formed a handy group for the discussion of such questions. By contrast, it is difficult to focus on a popularly identifiable species of corporation in Canada. A mere handful of corporations is known to the public — because it deals with them regularly. Generally speaking, these are the corporations most nearly identified with the marketplace and, hence, presumably are in the greatest need of corporate autonomy. Yet, their situation can not be taken as entirely typical when the question of corporate accountability is posed.

To a considerable degree, Parliament's level of corporate visibility appears to be no higher than the public's. In the question period and, to a lesser extent, in debates and in committees, the lion's share of attention goes to those few corporations in the public eye. There is, of course, nothing extraordinary about this, and it can be argued with much justification that the House of Commons serves its constituents best by concentrating on those governmental units in which there is the greatest interest. Furthermore, these corporations are, in general, the most important ones in the country from the standpoint of size and function. Granted all this, the question still arises of whether Parliament does not have the duty to be more systematic in approaching the task of holding corporations "ultimately accountable."

What is needed is not less attention to the corporations in question — they deserve all the attention they are getting — but more discipline on the part of the House in assuring itself of a comprehensive approach. Discipline is needed because it is natural to ignore those corporations which promise little in the way of political fruits. Several possibilities applicable to all of Parliament's accountability techniques may be outlined here. The present practice of having leading members of the opposition act as spokesmen on certain subjects and certain agencies might be extended to give

more detailed coverage to the work of unpublicized corporations. If the pressure of time forces a delegation of much
of this to opposition leaders-in-training, there are certain
obvious advantages to the process. In addition, staff assistance to opposition members probably should be provided
(giving technical assistance and research facilities to members of Parliament has been a widely recommended move
for some time).[4] Presumably, the result of systematic attention to all corporations would be a considerable improvement in the range and quality of discussion about
corporations. The question period and all types of debates
in which corporations can be discussed should take on a
more hardhitting quality. The present haphazard drive to
give more scrutiny to corporations in committees should
take on more direction.

Haphazard or not, an emphasis on committees as the principal tools for achieving systematic accountability seems
appropriate because they offer the best opportunity for expanding present efforts. The work of a few standing and
select committees with a handful of important or controversial corporations has indicated the possibilities. Real-
istically, however, it must be admitted that the likelihood
of Parliament undertaking to examine all corporations
through a series of standing or select committees is remote,
even if some extension may be anticipated in the future
and more should be encouraged. For the less prominent or
less well-known corporations, there are several other possibilities for more thorough review in committees than at
present. The Committee on Public Accounts might be in-
duced to adopt several suggestions — some its own — for
increasing its efficiency. These include annual meetings as
a matter of course, the establishment of subcommittees, concentration on selected corporations for more thorough review, and the assignment of the committee chairmanship to

a member of the opposition. The sense of futility that at times has pervaded the committee because it deals with past accounts rather than current expenditures might be partly overcome if a stronger attempt were made to relate information on past corporate actions to debates and questions in the House of Commons that deal with current activities. (The House's establishment of an estimates committee in 1955 to scrutinize in detail the estimates of about four governmental departments annually should also have lessened the committee's frustration.) If upon trial it was found that the pressure of other duties prevented members of the House of Commons from taking on the entire range of committee activities suggested above, the Senate might be pressed into service. Although its usefulness has often been questioned, the work of its committees has often been of considerable aid to the other chamber.[5]

Any proposal for increased committee activity immediately raises the question of whether the result might not be an intolerable degree of interference with corporate decision-making as well as a disruption of the pattern of ministerial responsibility. Certainly this is a legitimate fear. It had a basis in fact when government railways were operated by a government department up to 1919 and, to a lesser extent, when a large corporate board whose members had strong roots in local communities governed the Canadian National Railways. At present the situation appears to be that those few corporations about whose activities Parliament is most knowledgeable do not suffer seriously from overeager committee action, though for the C.N.R. there is some restraining effect (see Chapter 5). If it is true that thorough parliamentary knowledge has not led to stultifying control of the most entrepreneurial corporations, an extension of committee activity to other corporations may be viewed with some equanimity. On the positive side, the benefits from regularized committee investigations might be the following: (1) to remove parliamentary knowledge about specific corporations from the realm of the accidental; (2) to provide a two-way channel of communication by providing corporations with a forum and the committee with an opportunity for the transmission of parliamentary and public reaction about corporate activities; and (3) to recognize more adequately Parliament's legitimate interest as the representative of the taxpayers, who bear the ultimate risk of corporate operations. As to the last point, a familiar complaint of members of Parliament has been that those corporations that do not incur deficits escape the scrutiny of Parliament. Logically, the taxpayers' risk extends throughout the gamut of corporations and is not concentrated in those with a deficit.[6]

Undoubtedly, there is a fine line between encouraging corporations to learn the discipline of a balance sheet and judging the success of corporations by their balance sheets. The Canadian government has gone beyond the American in attempting to establish the discipline, but, in the process, it may also have veered closer to a "balance sheet mentality." In order to make their situation more truly comparable to private industry, proprietary corporations pay the federal income tax upon their net profits. On capital borrowed from the government, 96 per cent of the total advances are interest-bearing.[7] An effort is made to keep the interest rate and the terms of the borrowing by corporations at a level at least equal to the market rate for government securities of an equal term. In actuality, though these are sterner standards than American public corporations generally must meet, relatively few corporations fit the picture conjured up by these measures. Even when the dozen or so proprietary corporations are singled out, only about a third are producing and retaining substantial profits. The remainder show little promise of making significant contributions to their capital development programs. Of the three possible sources of money for government corporations — public funds, private investors, and corporate earnings — the first source is by far the greatest.[8] Yet, granting the limited applicability of the pure business image to public corporations, some corporate officials, judging by their published utterances, appear to find a stimulus toward greater corporate efforts in the language of the balance sheet. Even though an income tax on public corporations may amount to the government paying itself, if it has discipline value it is not to be rejected lightly. If all parties concerned can keep from making a fetish out of financial reports at the expense of a broader view of accountability, there would seem to be a good deal of merit in the notion of making the more "commercial" public corporations operate under conditions as closely resembling private business as possible.

Within limits, it can be argued that the desirability of a more systematic approach by Parliament to corporate supervision is reinforced by the fact that there exists a relatively strong system of corporate accountability to ministers. Systematic vigilance by Parliament over corporations then becomes more nearly a part of its responsibility to hold the government of the day accountable. The danger of parliamentary meddling in corporate affairs, on the other hand, is minimized by the fact that the government is always in a position to exert its own influence over the activities of corporations.

The web of ministerial controls over corporations would seem to be systematic to the same degree as the legislative controls are haphazard. (In a sense this statement is, of course, unfair to Parliament for it has authorized through statutes the very system employed by ministers.) Although the Governor in Council — rather than individual ministers, as in the United Kingdom — is normally empowered to act, the pattern of formal powers resembles the British system rather closely. Ministerial powers over corporations include appointment and dismissal, approval or disapproval of (mainly financial) actions, the requirement of reports, and, in some cases, the power to issue directives. The network of financial controls assigns responsibilities to ministers to whom corporations report, to the minister of finance, and to the Governor in Council. The apparent rigidity of such a system is strongly tempered by accommodating it to the needs of the various corporations through variations in the wording of organic statutes as well as the exceptions incorporated into the single over-all statute, the Financial Administration Act. In addition, formal relations are inevitably influenced by the informal give and take of daily dealings. The precise relation between a corporation and government officials naturally is the product of numerous variables, many of which are impossible for outsiders to identify. Such information about informal relations as is available does not suggest that the corporations, with perhaps a few notable exceptions, exercise much independence. True, the formal ministerial powers appear not to have been used a great deal. For example, even the Conservative victories of 1957 and 1958 have produced few immediate changes in the composition of corporate boards (except where new boards have replaced old ones, as for the Agricultural Stabilization Board and the Canadian Broadcasting Corporation). Furthermore, under the Liberals the power to issue general directions appears to have been used very sparingly. Actually, as several commentators have noted with respect to the British situation, inactivity in exercising formal powers does not necessarily indicate ministerial indifference to corporate action. Informal means are always available as channels of communication. Everything about the Canadian situation points to a close working relation between ministries and corporations. Granted that differences exist, it is apparent, as we have seen, that consultation plays an important part in department-corporation relations. In the intimacy of government circles in Ottawa, first-name relations are common — and the corporations are no exception to the rule. In addition, interested departments may have representatives on corporate boards. Even where they do not, the executive heads of corporations have sometimes been former members of the departmental bureaucracy or have been associated with department heads in the past. Finally, the fact that few corporations deal directly with the public or must meet the demands of market conditions accentuates the degree of their association with departments. Consumers' councils and joint consultation are not used in Canada, as was noted. Advisory committees, though important to the work of some corporations, are not very widely employed. In short, relatively few situations are found where conditions making for corporate independence are so prevalent as to create a genuine dilemma about a corporation's place in the scheme of things.

Does a pattern of strong ministerial controls over corporations intensify or simplify the problem of corporate accountability? In the absence of such controls, Parliament might be constantly tempted to interfere in management decisions. With the knowledge that the controls exist, Parliament tends to rely on the ministers in holding the corporations accountable. This reasoning may account for the fact that Parliament has not expressed more opposition to departmental membership on corporate boards. Especially with respect to Crown companies, members of Parliament have in fact actually asked whether it would "not give parliament more security and the government a better opportunity to maintain control of the moneys spent if it were represented on the boards of these companies?" In the same vein it has been argued that "If the minister has some direct tie-up with the board it brings parliament that much closer to it." [9] It is significant that the conventional answer ministers have given to such comments is that without themselves sitting on boards, they have numerous controls at hand to prevent corporations from being irresponsible. From the point of view of the government of the day strong ministerial controls undoubtedly simplify the problem of accountability.

Yet, despite the comfort Parliament may take from the knowledge that ministerial links to corporations are strong, it has reason to doubt that the problem of accountability has been simplified. As one commentator has said about the parallel British action in strengthening ministerial controls over the nationalized industries, as compared with earlier corporations: "In a sense, this exaggerated the problem of public accountability, for it is one thing to create a public trust which is to all intents, independent of the Government of the day, and over which Parliament has little control; it is another to create a public corporation immediately responsible to a minister of the Crown for a multitude of matters, and then to deny Parliament the right to control the minister." [10] It is a fact in Canada, as in Britain, that, substantial as the ministerial controls may be, they leave sufficient discretion to corporations to permit ministers to disclaim knowledge of, or control over, various corporate actions. Both countries follow the rule that corporations — in the words of Herbert Morrison — "are accountable to Parliament through Ministers on the matters for which Ministers are themselves responsible." [11] Though this may be sound governmental doctrine, it sometimes leaves the legislature with an acute sense of frustration. Perennial disputes over the proper subject matter of questions asked about corporations have plagued the Canadian Parliament as well as the British. As the latter legislature, even with the aid of the speaker's impartial judgment, has not been able to establish clear-cut criteria for the untouchable but vague area of day-to-day administration, it is logical to expect a continuation of the confusion over the topic in Canada. Frustration may also be the result of floor debates on the subject of corporations. As Prime Minister Diefenbaker stated in exasperation at a time when his was the opposition party: "In my opinion there is no proper examination possible in parliament of overexpenditure by crown corporations." [12] And again, in more precise terms: "Whenever they need money they come to parliament, but whenever we endeavour to ascertain whether they have overexpended or recklessly wasted, then they hide behind the fiction that parliament has no right to know." [13] As to Parliament's third accountability device, although more system can (and should) be introduced into committee investigations, it is unrealistic to expect that Parliament would be completely reassured about its knowledge of corporate actions. Finally, though Parliament may have been too lenient in, for example, giving the Governor in Council authority to establish subsidiary Crown companies or in not requiring annual reports of corporations to record instances of ministers' use of the power of giving general directions, a tightening up of such requirements would not totally dispel Parliament's feeling of remoteness from the corporations. In short, Parliament can allay its uneasiness by informing itself more fully, but, short of decreeing the end of existing corporate independence, it can expect a certain amount of frustration over the problem of accountability.

Taking into account the considerable variety that exists, Canadian public corporations appear to have found an acceptable niche in the governmental system. In the Canadian formula accountability is dominant, but corporate freedom is far from extinct. This is in accord with current trends in certain other Western countries and, what is more important, with the basic tenets of the parliamentary system. Aside from obtaining more energy and consistency in Parliament's approach to corporations, however, further standardization of controls would not seem to be warranted. Pursued further, the result might be the loss of the essential qualities for which corporations have been created. At the very least, the historical intercorporate differences that are a legitimate feature of a pragmatic nation would suffer. If this statement emphasizes the extent to which the Canadian system of corporate accountability was devised for a particular set of conditions, it should, nevertheless, not be taken as skepticism about the adaptability of elements of the system to other countries.

Chapter 1

PRAGMATISM AND PUBLIC ENTERPRISE

1. J. E. Hodgetts, "The Public Corporation in Canada," in *The Public Corporation,* ed. Wolfgang Friedmann (Toronto, 1954), pp. 56–58. Two of the second group of agencies have been liquidated.

2. *Statutes of Canada,* 15–16 Geo. VI, c. 12 (2d sess., 1951). Part VIII applies to corporations. It should be noted that the operation of this part of the act is limited by (1) the supremacy of other statutes in case of conflict; and (2) the exclusion of six corporations.

3. Three were excluded because they are joint dominion-provincial boards: Eastern Rockies Forest Conservation Board, Halifax Relief Commission, and Northern Ontario Pipe Line Crown Corporation. Of the other three, the Canadian Wheat Board was excluded because "it is in fact regarded more as an agent of the farmer or grain producer than of the Crown," and the Bank of Canada and its subsidiary, the Industrial Development Bank, because of their special character. See Standing Committee on Public Accounts, *Minutes of Proceedings and Evidence,* 1951, 2d sess., pp. 101–103.

4. *Revised Statutes of Canada* (1952), c. 116, Schedules B, C, and D. Subsequent changes noted through interviews.

5. H. R. Balls, "The Financial Control and Accountability of Canadian Crown Corporations," *Public Administration,* XXXI (Summer 1953), 127–143, at 130.

6. Proprietary corporations escape from the following provisions: "Each agency corporation shall annually submit to the appropriate Minister an operating budget . . . for the approval of the appropriate Minister and the Minister of Finance" (Section 80[1]). "The Governor in Council may make regulations with respect to the conditions upon which an agency corporation may undertake contractual commitments" (Section 83). Proprietary as well as agency corporations are required to submit capital budgets for approval.

7. Frank A. Milligan, "Financing the Canadian Crown Corporations: General Financial Provisions," Seminar Paper No. 67 (mimeo.), Seminar on Organization and Administration of Public Enterprises in the Industrial Field, Rangoon, Burma, March 1954, p. 5. A condensation of this and other seminar papers appears in *Public Enterprise: A Study of Its Organization and Management in Various Countries,* ed. A. H. Hanson (Brussels, 1955).

8. From the standpoint of ownership, one other intercountry difference may be noted in passing. Canada has not deliberately created mixed-ownership corporations (such as the Federal National

147

Mortgage Association and certain others in the credit field) nor has it any procedure whereby private persons purchase stock in a public corporation with which they do business. It is true, however, that borrowings from the public are authorized for a number of Canadian corporations. Only three have actually borrowed by the public sale of securities, namely, the Canadian National Railways, Canadian National (West Indies) Steamships Limited, and the Canadian Wheat Board. See Frank A. Milligan, "Financing the Canadian Crown Corporations: Capital Financing," Seminar Paper No. 69 (see n. 6 above).

9. "The State and Economic Life," in *Canada,* ed. George W. Brown (Berkeley, 1950), p. 353.

10. Maurice Lamontagne, "The Role of Government," in *Canada's Tomorrow,* ed. G. P. Gilmour (Toronto, 1954), p. 122.

11. The term was popularized by MacDonald and the Conservatives in the campaign of 1878. Its meaning is generally restricted to the institution of the protective tariff, but cogent arguments have been made for subsuming the entire group of policies named above under the title. See V. C. Fowke, "The National Policy — Old and New," *Canadian Journal of Economics and Political Science,* XVIII (August 1952), 271–286, and Brady, "The State and Economic Life," in *Canada,* pp. 358–359.

12. Brady, in *Canada,* p. 353.

13. *Debates,* House of Commons (hereafter referred to as *Debates*), 1937, p. 2215.

14. *Debates,* 1945, 2d sess., p. 1358. A member of the opposition responded with further words of praise "for what they [T.C.A.] have done in helping to develop the country" (p. 1359).

15. *Debates,* 1932, pp. 3035–36.

16. In 1950, under the stimulus of an agreement concluded by the Commonwealth countries, the Canadian Overseas Telecommunication Corporation did expropriate (under the direction of the Governor in Council) the facilities of two private companies engaged in external telecommunications. See the corporation's first *Annual Report,* dated March 31, 1951.

17. *Debates,* 1917, p. 4218.

18. *Ibid.,* p. 4015.

19. *Debates,* 1919, p. 1741.

20. *Ibid.,* 2d sess., p. 1054.

21. *Debates,* 1917, pp. 4275, 4384; and 1919, 2d sess., p. 1057.

22. *Debates,* 1917, p. 4015. It is true that the M.P.s' awareness of public ownership sentiment produced an almost ludicrous jockeying to gain credit for public ownership measures while denying a doctrinaire bias toward the principle (see pp. 1811 and 2115). Furthermore, several prominent Conservatives seem to have expected pub-

lic ownership to play an increasingly important role as the industrialization of Canada proceeded.

23. J. L. Ilsley, the minister of finance, argued as follows. "The house will appreciate, however, that unlike the industrial development bank, which will operate with a relatively few offices and a comparatively small but highly skilled staff, a similar agency to provide intermediate credit for agriculture could do its job effectively only with literally thousands of branches or offices throughout rural areas readily accessible to farmers. Some of the United States farm credit organizations were considered as possible models, but . . . the same objective could be attained more speedily and effectively and at a fraction of the cost by a comparatively simple extension of existing lending facilities. Moreover, a new set of institutions would have taken years to build up and to equip with competent and experienced staff." *Debates*, 1944, p. 2558.

24. *Ibid.*, p. 2547.

25. *Ibid.*, p. 2718.

26. See the "White Paper" issued by C. D. Howe, the minister of reconstruction and development in 1945 (*Employment and Income, with Special Reference to the Initial Period of Reconstruction*, Ottawa, 1945); an article by Howe, "Industrial Development in Canada," *Public Affairs*, XI (December 1948), 207–213, in which the author lists "four principles underlying our industrial development program"; and O. J. Firestone, "Investment and Economic Development in Canada," *The Statist* (Canadian Supplement), (May 31, 1952) pp. 18–20. For an indication of the extent to which business regards itself as a partner of government, see John T. Bryden, "Government and Business," in *Canada: Nation on the March* (Toronto, 1953), pp. 67–74, and Howard Gamble, "The Road to Tomorrow," *Canadian Business*, XXVII (January 1954), 22–24, 50ff. Gamble asserts, "There is in Canada probably a greater genuine liaison and rapport between government and business than in any other country" (p. 50).

27. The Minister was authorized by statute to procure the incorporation of Crown companies under the federal Companies Act, 1934, or provincial companies acts — all statutes designed for the use of private corporations. Twenty-eight companies were created under the authority given the Minister. See J. de N. Kennedy, *History of the Department of Munitions and Supply*, 2 vols. (Ottawa, 1950). A few Crown companies survived the war, and authorization to create others has been given to several agencies since the war. The word "Limited" in the title identifies this special type of public corporation.

28. *Debates*, 1946, p. 2176.

29. *Ibid.*, p. 1517.

30. See *Disposal and Peacetime Use of Crown Plant Buildings,* Department of Reconstruction and Supply (Ottawa, 1948), p. 3.

31. *Debates,* 1944, p. 1573.

32. Address by C. D. Howe, Minister of Trade and Commerce and Minister of Defence Production, Los Angeles, California, Oct. 8, 1954 (press release).

33. Compare the instituting of competition between public corporations in the fuel industry by the British Conservative Government. Ernest Davies, "Government Policy and the Public Corporation," *Political Quarterly,* XXVI (April-June 1955), 104–116.

34. *Debates,* 1917, p. 4217.

35. *Debates,* 1919, p. 2110.

36. The words were used in a speech broadcast to the nation from Winnipeg. Quoted in *Debates,* 1932–33, p. 2800.

37. Harold A. Innis, *Political Economy in the Modern State* (Toronto, 1946), pp. 159–160.

38. *Debates,* 1919, p. 1018.

39. For example, speaking of the successful government ventures in synthetic rubber production and uranium mining and refining, the Minister of Defence Production asserted ". . . if they did not have monopolies they would be crown companies in a competitive field, which is contrary to government policy." *Debates,* 1951, p. 2004. See also *Debates,* 1946, p. 2176.

40. "The government has no intention of going into business unnecessarily. Occasions have arisen in the past where it was important and, I suggest, imperative, that the government go into business on a very large scale. Such occasions may occur again, and if they do I hope the government of that day will be bold enough to meet the situation." C. D. Howe, minister of reconstruction and supply, *Debates,* 1946, p. 1517.

41. An illustration is found in a colloquy between C. D. Howe and the present Conservative Prime Minister that occurred while Polymer Corporation was under discussion (*Debates,* 1944, p. 1715):

> "Mr. Howe: 'With what private industry does it compete?'
> Mr. Diefenbaker: 'It does not compete in the matter of manufacture, true enough, but it is actually the first move along the road to socialization.'
> Mr. Howe: 'It is a wholly non-competitive industry.'
> Mr. Diefenbaker: 'That is true.'"

42. For a statement of the association's case, see Special Committee on Broadcasting, *Minutes of Proceedings and Evidence,* 1952–53, pp. 252–292, 311–317.

43. See Royal Commission on National Development in the Arts, Letters and Sciences, *Report* (Ottawa, 1951).

44. Royal Commission on Broadcasting, *Report*, 2 vols. (Ottawa, 1957). The body of the report is contained in vol. I.

45. Bill C–55, An Act respecting Broadcasting, as passed by the House of Commons, 26th August, 1958, First Session, Twenty-Fourth Parliament, 7 Elizabeth II, 1958.

46. *Debates*, 1958, pp. 4077 and 4108, respectively.

47. A. W. Currie, *Economics of Canadian Transportation* (Toronto, 1954), p. 544.

48. Speech at Timmins, Ontario, Feb. 7, 1958, reported in *Canadian Weekly Bulletin*, XIII, No. 8, Feb. 19, 1958 (Dept. of External Affairs, Ottawa).

49. *Debates*, 1952–53, p. 3548.

50. One of the declared aims of Public Law 108 (83d Cong., 1st sess.), which established the commission, was the elimination of "non-essential services, functions, and activities which are competitive with private enterprise." 67 Stat. 142 (1953).

51. *Ottawa Journal*, Jan. 24, 1955, p. 6.

52. See, for example, Royal Commission on Transportation, *Report* (Ottawa, 1951), pp. 193–194; *Debates*, 1923, p. 1616; and 1932–33, p. 2771; and R. J. Manion, *Life Is an Adventure* (Toronto, 1936), p. 295.

53. Hodgetts, in *The Public Corporation*, p. 54.

54. *Debates*, 1923, p. 3674.

55. *Debates*, 1921, p. 1182.

56. A point amply demonstrated by the harassed Liberal Minister of Railways and Canals, when he said in the House: "Suppose Mr. Beatty's shareholders met and stayed in session four or five months every year; suppose every day a portion of his staff was compelled to be taken from their work to answer all kinds of questions; suppose that . . . among his shareholders there was a large number who made no bones about declaring him and his board of management incompetent; what would Mr. Beatty do? He would resign in five minutes." *Debates*, 1924, pp. 2632–33.

57. *Statutes of Canada*, 1 Eliz. II, c. 29 (1952). The provision was an amendment to the Income Tax Act, *Statutes of Canada*, 11–12 Geo. VI, c. 52 (1948), which had provided in section 57 (1) (d) for exemption of "a corporation, commission, or association not less than 90% of the shares or capital of which was owned by His Majesty in right of Canada or a province or by a Canadian municipality."

58. See, for example, *Debates*, 1946, pp. 1517, 2129, and 2150.

59. *Debates*, 1952, p. 1253. The amounts paid by each eligible corporation can be ascertained quickly from their financial statements, which are published annually in Volume II of the *Public Accounts of Canada*.

60. *Debates*, 1952, p. 2093.

61. In November, 1949, Minister of Finance Douglas Abbott announced to the House that "in general the policy of the government will be to authorize its Crown corporations to work out fair and equitable agreements with the municipalities in which their properties are situated." *Debates*, 1949, 2d sess., p. 1706. In June, 1951, the Minister used stronger language to describe the situation, saying that the corporations had been "instructed" to negotiate agreements. *Debates*, 1951, p. 4217. The reason given by the Minister for permitting each corporation to work out its own "fair and equitable" agreements was that "the character of the operations of these Crown corporations varies a good deal" (p. 4224).

62. See *Debates*, 1945, p. 1424; and 1946, pp. 1517, 2129, 2148, 2163. The cities have no legal recourse if a corporation refuses to conclude such an arrangement. There has not been complete satisfaction with the size of the payments. See, for example, *Debates*, 1951, p. 4226.

63. *Debates*, 1952, p. 2092.

64. *Ibid.*, p. 1253. The relief granted "will take the form of a deduction from the tax otherwise payable of an amount sufficient to reduce to 43 per cent the tax payable under the Income Tax Act on that part of a corporation's taxable income that is derived from such distribution or generation." At the 1952 corporate income tax rate of 50 per cent, the reduction amounted to 14 per cent.

65. *Ibid.*, p. 2645. Earlier, in response to complaints that provinces with privately owned public utility companies were being discriminated against because publicly owned companies in other provinces paid no federal income taxes, the federal government had arranged to turn over to a province half of the income tax collected from such private companies within its borders. This step and the 1952 reduction were regarded as parallel moves.

66. W. A. Mackintosh, "The People and Their History," in *Canada: Nation on the March*, p. 18.

67. For example, in commenting on the loss of 28 million dollars suffered by the Canadian National Railways in 1954 under Liberal auspices, a Conservative newspaper pointed to the reduction of 32 million dollars in operating expenses as proof that the loss "was not helped by failure on the part of management to economize." Falling revenues were blamed, and it was acknowledged that "it is not always possible to match falling revenues with cuts in costs." The railroad's plans for meeting competition were noted. Editorial, *Ottawa Journal*, March 23, 1955, p. 6. Earlier, in referring to the anticipated loss, the president of the C.N.R. was reported as viewing it as a "crushing disappointment," particularly because making a profit is essential for a public corporation. "Exhortations from an executive officer are a

poor substitute for the discipline of a profit and loss account."
Ottawa Journal, Nov. 4, 1954, p. 38.

68. *Debates*, 1945, p. 1397. Behind this statement is another made
by Howe on a different occasion: "We in Canada have always had to
live by compromise. . . ." Address at Case Institute of Technology,
Cleveland, April 10, 1953 (press release).

69. *Debates*, 1952–53, p. 4764.

Chapter 2

THE ROOTS OF ACCOUNTABILITY

1. See, for example, *Public Enterprise: A Study of Its Organization and Management in Various Countries*, ed. A. H. Hanson (Brussels, 1955); *The Public Corporation: A Comparative Symposium*, ed.
Wolfgang Friedmann (Toronto, 1954); Temporary State Commission
on Coordination of State Activities, *Staff Report on Public Authorities
under New York State*, Leg. Doc. No. 46 (Albany, 1956).

2. G. N. Ostergaard, "Labour and the Development of the Public
Corporation," *Manchester School of Economic and Social Studies*,
XXII (May 1954), 192–226, at 193.

3. Eldon L. Johnson, "The Accountability of the British Nationalized Industries," *American Political Science Review*, XLVIII (June
1954), 366–385, at 367.

4. Ostergaard, pp. 203–204.

5. The earliest public corporations established under auspices of
the Canadian government probably were the various harbor commissions, the first of which was established for Montreal in 1852. The
harbor commissioners and their successors were named "a Body
Corporate and Politic" and given powers, among other things, to acquire vessels. See *Statutes of Canada*, 16 Vict., c. 24 (1852). The
oldest existing corporation is the National Battlefields Commission
(1908), although the predecessor of the Federal District Commission, the Ottawa Improvement Commission, was established in 1899.
Other corporations created before 1919 were the National Gallery
of Canada (1913) and the Halifax Relief Commission (1918).

6. *Debates*, 1919, p. 1414.

7. *Ibid.*, p. 1625.

8. J. D. Reid, minister of railways and canals, stated: "The reason
why it is left to the Governor in Council is because the people are
the shareholders, and the shareholders are the ones who elect the
directors and fix their salaries." *Ibid.*, p. 1414.

9. *Ibid.*, p. 1624.

10. A. W. Currie, *Economics of Canadian Transportation* (Toronto, 1954), p. 440.

11. An example was given by the Minister of Railways and Canals: "I will tell you what happened on the Intercolonial railway during the past few years . . . We have in Nova Scotia one or two mines where the coal is much more valuable than that produced from other mines . . . Years ago a difference was allowed for this coal, because of its quality. A question was asked each year and the information given to the public as to the prices that the Government were paying for the coal. Political influence came in each year . . . with the result . . . that we are paying just as much for coal that is not of this high quality as we are for the high-quality article." *Debates,* 1919, p. 1641.

12. The rationale of the Minister of Railways and Canals was as follows: "No matter what minister may be operating that line there will always be a difference of opinion between him and the patrons of the road, and I think we should have this safeguard, especially as it looks as though the Government were going into further government ownership. Therefore, the more independently those government lines can be operated, the better it will be in the interests of the country. *Debates,* 1917, p. 4340.

13. *Debates,* 1921, p. 1181.

14. *Ibid.,* p. 1183.

15. *Debates,* 1924, p. 2695.

16. *Debates,* 1921, p. 1183.

17. Information acquired, said the Minister of Railways and Canals, might be used to injure public ownership, create trouble between public and private railway companies, or for personal monetary advantage. *Debates,* 1920, p. 4195.

18. *Ibid.,* p. 1670.

19. *Debates,* 1921, p. 1178. The only reservation was one that is conventionally understood as applying to the question hour and the production of documents, namely, "that in exceptional cases there may be documents of a confidential character which, in the public interest, may properly be withheld from publication."

20. For this their opponents taunted them often. See, for example, *Debates,* 1924, pp. 2692–95.

21. *Debates,* 1919, 2d sess., p. 1207.

22. *Debates,* 1919, p. 1634.

23. *Ibid.,* p. 1397.

24. *Debates,* 1921, p. 1808. The quotation is from a newspaper editorial read to the House by a Liberal member.

25. *Debates,* 1919, p. 1398.

26. *Ibid.,* p. 1704.

27. *Ibid.,* p. 1634.

28. *Debates,* 1921, p. 1181.

29. *Debates,* 1919, p. 1703.

30. *Debates,* 1922, p. 881.

31. *Debates,* 1923, p. 3673.

32. *Ibid.,* pp. 3673–74.

33. The Borden government was waging a strong battle for civil service reform at the very time acquisition of the private railroads was being debated. The Civil Service Act of 1918, as amended, is still the basic statute upon which the powers of the Civil Service Commission rest. See Taylor Cole, *The Canadian Bureaucracy* (Durham, N.C., 1949), p. 11.

34. In speaking of the acquisition of the Canadian Northern, the first of the systems transferred to government control, Prime Minister Sir Robert Borden told the House: "By acquiring the stock without taking the property out of the ownership of the company we still use the corporate machinery, the staff of employees, all the organization that has been built up during fifteen or twenty years." *Debates,* 1917, p. 4481. The Minister of Finance was persuaded that "The chief advantage of preserving the corporate identity of all the companies embraced in the system is that it maintains the financing which is already being done and it facilitates future financing . . ." *Ibid.,* p. 4223.

35. In explaining the Canadian National Railways Bill in 1919, the Minister of Railways and Canals stated that "The different railways owned by the Government have different ways of collecting revenue and making expenditures, and it is necessary to get one uniform system." *Debates,* 1919, p. 1397.

36. In drafting the Canadian National Railways measure, the Minister of Railways and Canals confessed to "taking as a model the charter of a privately owned company like the Canadian Pacific railway, and altering it as necessary to make it applicable to a Government owned railway." *Ibid.,* p. 1396.

37. *Robert Laird Borden: His Memoirs,* ed. Henry Borden, II, 653.

38. As constituted by its organic statute of 1906, the commission "was designed to be in law a body corporate but comformable in broad essentials to a department of the government." Alexander Brady, "The Ontario Hydro-Electric Power Commission," *Canadian Journal of Economics and Political Science,* II (August 1936), 331–353, at 331. Between 1906 and 1925, under the dynamic leadership of its chairman, Sir Adam Beck, the commission became "something difficult to define, but essentially different from a department of the government. The government was still the banker, providing the money for all important extensions, but in no close way endeavouring

to scrutinize the internal management of the Commission in its expenditures, and offering guarantees to support the Commission's credit without requiring the approval of the Legislature." *Ibid.*, p. 337.

39. *Debates*, 1951, 2d sess., p. 1371.

40. These included the National Research Council (1924), Federal District Commission (1927), Federal Farm Loan Board (1927), and a subsidiary of the C.N.R., Canadian National (West Indies) Steamships Limited (1927).

41. See, for example, John J. Deutsch, "Parliament and the Civil Service: Can the Complex Be Controlled?" *Queen's Quarterly*, XLIII (Winter 1957), 565–573.

42. *Revised Statutes of Canada* (1952), c. 53. "In addition to the provisions of the Companies Act itself there are three other legal instruments that determine the operation of these companies. An Order in Council is the creative instrument; Letters Patent issued by the Secretary of State provide the legal authorization for the company to do business under the Companies Act; and the formal agreement between the company and the minister sets out in detail the structure, financing and powers of the agency." Hodgetts, in *The Public Corporation*, ed. W. Friedmann, p. 59.

43. *Statutes of Canada*, 17 Geo. V, c. 29 (1927).

44. *Statutes of Canada*, 3 Geo. VI, c. 31 (1940). See also Balls, "Financial Control," *Public Administration*, XXXI, 129.

45. Watson Sellar, "Crown Munitions Companies," *Canadian Chartered Accountant*, XLII (June 1943), 402–409, at 403.

46. Kennedy, *History of the Department of Munitions and Supply*, I, 286. A half-dozen other Crown companies were created under other wartime legislation, but the Companies Act again was invoked. See Balls, "Financial Control," *Public Administration*, XXXI, 129.

47. Sellar, 403.

48. *Debates*, 1946, p. 1512.

49. See, for example, *Debates*, 1942, pp. 3204–06, and *Debates*, 1943, p. 416.

50. In the postwar period authorization for using the Crown company plan was granted in the Defence Production Act, Atomic Energy Control Act, and in an amendment to the Research Council Act.

51. *Statutes of Canada*, 10 Geo. VI, c. 24 (1946).

52. Balls, "Financial Control," *Public Administration*, XXXI, 130.

Chapter 3

THE SUPERVISORS

1. *Statutes of Canada,* 15–16 Geo. VI, c. 12, s. 76 (1951, 2d sess.).

2. This term is used in preference to the word "Cabinet" because properly speaking that term is applied to the Committee of the Privy Council only in its policy-making capacity. "Council" is used in this chapter as a short reference to "Governor in Council."

3. Hodgetts, "The Public Corporation in Canada," *Public Administration,* XXVIII, 286.

4. *Revised Statutes of Canada* (1952), c. 13, s. 9.

5. *Revised Statutes of Canada* (1952), c. 46, ss. 6, 7, 8. Although the statute refers to the Minister of Resources and Development as the supervising minister, the corporation now reports to the Minister of Public Works.

6. *Statutes of Canada,* 11 Geo. VI, c. 59, s. 4 (1947).

7. *Statutes of Canada,* 7–8 Ed. VII, c. 57, s. 1 (1908). Quebec and Ontario at present have members on the Commission.

8. *Statutes of Canada,* 4–5 Eliz. II, c. 10, s. 3 (1956).

9. Exchange of letters between Hon. C. D. Howe, minister of trade and commerce, and Hon. Dana Porter, treasurer of Ontario, dated November 21 and 22, 1955, respectively, constituting an agreement. In sessional paper no. 174–B, tabled February 21, 1956. Parliamentary Papers Branch, House of Commons, Ottawa.

10. *Revised Statutes of Canada* (1952), c. 112, s. 3.

11. *Revised Statutes of Canada* (1952), c. 268, s. 5.

12. *Revised Statutes of Canada* (1952), c. 39, ss. 7, 8. See also, testimony of C. D. Howe, Sessional Committee on Railways and Shipping, *Minutes of Proceedings and Evidence,* 1951, p. 236.

13. *Statutes of Canada,* 4–5 Eliz. II, c. 25, s. 2 (1956). This statute deleted reference to the assistant deputy governor as a member. His office was actually eliminated two years earlier.

14. Atomic Energy of Canada Limited, Canadian Arsenals Limited, Canadian National (West Indies) Steamships Limited, Canadian Patents and Development Limited, Defence Construction (1951) Limited, Eldorado Aviation Limited, Eldorado Mining and Refining Limited, Northern Transportation Company Limited, Park Steamship Company Limited, and Polymer Corporation Limited.

15. *Revised Statutes of Canada* (1952), c. 62.

16. *Statutes of Canada,* 2–3 Eliz. II, c. 47, s. 4 (1954). The minister in this case is the chairman of the Committee of the Privy Council on Scientific and Industrial Research or else a designee of the Governor in Council. The portfolio was held by C. D. Howe under the Liberals.

17. *Revised Statutes of Canada* (1952), c. 239, s. 17.

18. For the first eight years of its existence, the Canadian Farm Loan Board operated under a system whereby borrowers were required to subscribe to capital stock to an amount equal to 5 per cent of the sum borrowed. They were, however, given no power to choose members of the board. *Statutes of Canada,* 17 Geo. V, c. 43, s. 5 (1927).

19. *Debates,* 1944, pp. 1571–72.

20. *Statutes of Canada,* 24–25 Geo. V, c. 43, s. 9 (1934).

21. *Debates,* 1936, p. 3264.

22. *Debates,* 1936, p. 3606. For the terms of the act, see *Statutes of Canada,* 1 Ed. VIII, c. 22 (1936).

23. *Debates,* 1938, p. 4056. For the terms of the act, see *Statutes of Canada,* 2 Geo. VI, c. 42 (1938).

24. Johnson, "The Accountability of the British Nationalized Industries," *American Political Science Review,* XLVIII, 369.

25. *Statutes of Canada,* 8–9 Geo. VI, c. 21 (1944–45).

26. When the statute was amended in 1949 and the name of the corporation was changed to Crown Assets Disposal Corporation, Section 10 was renumbered as Section 6 but retained virtually intact. Section 12 was repealed and a new section created to replace it, but the essence of the phrase quoted above was retained in the new section. *Statutes of Canada,* 13 Geo. VI, c. 38 (1949, 2d sess.).

27. *Statutes of Canada,* 10 Geo. VI, c. 40 (1946). The other statute made the Atomic Energy Control Board, created by the statute, subject to the directions of the Committee of the Privy Council on Scientific and Industrial Research rather than to the Governor in Council or a single minister. *Statutes of Canada,* 10 Geo. VI, c. 37, s. 7 (1946). In 1954 the act was amended to make the board subject to the directions of "the Minister," defined as the chairman of the Committee of the Privy Council on Scientific and Industrial Research. *Statutes of Canada,* 2–3 Eliz. II, c. 47, ss. 1, 3 (1954).

28. The citations, respectively, are *Statutes of Canada,* 11–12 Geo. VI, c. 64 (1948); 13 Geo. VI, c. 10 (1949, 2d sess.); and 14–15 Geo. VI, c. 24 (1951).

29. Making the Atomic Energy Control Board subject to the directions of a committee (see n. 27, above) served as a convenient substitute for the usual arrangement. Making the board subject to the directions of the chairman of the committee (in 1954) was still not equivalent to the British arrangement.

30. It is true that the three statutes that came after 1946 did not stipulate the type of directions. Nevertheless, as the phrase "any directions" is used in these statutes, inclusion of special directions is

a reasonable construction. For a brief summary of the wording in the British statutes, see Acton Society Trust, *The Powers of the Minister* (Claygate, 1951), p. 17.

31. *Debates,* 1951, p. 4284.

32. For example, to expedite the importation of monkeys needed for experiments with Salk vaccine, corporation officials suggested that the Minister of Health write to the Minister of Defence Production requesting him to direct the corporation to procure the monkeys. The request was even drafted by officials of the corporation.

33. Under the Liberals, four of the six corporations reported to C. D. Howe in his various capacities. Only one of the six is a departmental corporation while two are in the agency group and three are proprietary corporations. How much significance should be attached to these facts it is difficult to say.

34. There is no requirement for disclosure in annual reports of use of the ministerial directive, as in the case of the British nationalized industries.

35. The St. Lawrence Seaway Authority Act does require the authority to "comply with any direction not inconsistent with this Act" given by the Governor in Council for the purpose of ensuring compliance with Canada's international obligations. *Statutes of Canada,* 15–16, Geo. VI, c. 24, s. 20 (2d sess., 1951). The absence of the directive power in the Northern Ontario Pipe Line Crown Corporation Act, *Statutes of Canada,* 4–5 Eliz. II, c. 10 (1956), may perhaps be accounted for by the anticipation of provincial membership on the board of the corporation.

36. For the list of unclassified corporations, see Ch. 1, n. 3. The names of these corporations were omitted from the list of departmental, agency, and proprietary corporations in Schedules B, C, and D of the Act. Actually, although the Northern Ontario Pipe Line Crown Corporation is among the six omitted corporations, the act under which it was created makes a number of the sections in Part VIII of the Financial Administration Act applicable to the corporation. See *Statutes of Canada,* 4–5 Eliz. II, c. 10 (1956).

37. See *Statutes of Canada,* 15–16 Geo. VI, c. 12, ss. 87, 88 (1951, 2d sess.).

38. See Standing Committee on Public Accounts, *Minutes of Proceedings and Evidence,* 1951, 2d sess., p. 128.

39. Either the special statutes or the Governor in Council has in the past set fiscal year-ends, and in all cases of corporations in the agency or proprietary category either December 31 or March 31 has been used. The committee hearings on the act make it plain that the calendar year is to be preferred because it will "enable the

results of the operations of the corporation for a financial period to be incorporated in the public accounts" and because it avoids conflict with the date when the government must close its books. See *ibid.*, p. 108. See also Balls, "Financial Control," *Public Administration*, XXXI, 134.

40. Balls, "Financial Control," *Public Administration*, XXXI, 135.

41. See, for example, the Surplus Crown Assets Act, *Revised Statutes of Canada* (1952), c. 260, s. 11. For an account of an incident involving this statute see Standing Committee on Public Accounts, *Minutes of Proceedings and Evidence*, 1956, p. 91.

42. Frank A. Milligan, "Financing the Canadian Crown Corporation: General Financial Provisions," Seminar Paper No. 67 (mimeo.), Seminar on Organization and Administration of Public Enterprises in the Industrial Field, Rangoon, Burma, March 1954, p. 5. (See Chapter 1, n. 6, above.)

43. Balls, "Financial Control," *Public Administration*, XXXI, p. 139.

44. *Revised Statutes of Canada* (1952), c. 242.

45. Bill C–55, An Act respecting Broadcasting, as passed by the House of Commons, 26th August 1958, First Session, Twenty-Fourth Parliament. 7 Elizabeth II, 1958. Before 1958 the requirements were somewhat stricter. See *Revised Statutes of Canada* (1952), c. 32.

46. *Revised Statutes of Canada* (1952), c. 32, s. 23. In the 1958 statute, An Act respecting Broadcasting, the corporation was directed to report *to* the minister.

47. *Debates*, 1955, p. 1803.

48. *Revised Statutes of Canada* (1952), c. 39, ss. 14 (1), 15.

49. *Revised Statutes of Canada* (1952), c. 39, s. 16.

50. *Revised Statutes of Canada* (1952), c. 40, s. 33.

51. *Revised Statutes of Canada* (1952), c. 39, s. 12.

52. Balls, "Financial Control," *Public Administration*, XXXI, pp. 130–131, quoted by permission of the Hon. Editor, D. N. Chester.

53. See, for example, *Debates*, 1956, p. 4905.

54. See, for example, *Debates*, 1953–54, pp. 1065–66.

55. *Debates*, 1955, p. 1901. This was after a Conservative critic had pointed out similarities in the wording of the Minister's and the C.B.C.'s public statements (pp. 1892–94).

56. *Debates*, 1934, p. 4151.

57. *Ibid.*, p. 840.

58. *Ibid.*, p. 4226.

59. *Ibid.*, pp. 4235–36.

60. *Ibid.*, p. 4228.

61. *Debates*, 1941, p. 3936.

62. Standing Committee on Banking and Commerce, *Proceedings . . . Decennial Revision of the Bank Act*, 1954, pp. 25–26.

63. Bank of Canada, *Annual Report of the Governor for 1957,* p. 15.

64. Corporations usually decline to reveal publicly the results of consultation. When the commissioner of the Canadian Farm Loan Board was asked in committee whether the board agreed with the Liberal government's proposal to amend the statute under which the board operates, he replied: "The government, before it made this policy, consulted us. Further than that I do not think we can say anything." Standing Committee on Banking and Commerce, *Minutes of Proceedings and Evidence,* 1956, p. 177.

65. *Ibid.,* p. 138.

66. *Revised Statutes of Canada* (1952), c. 13, s. 20.

67. Standing Committee on Banking and Commerce, *Proceedings . . . Decennial Revision of the Bank Act,* 1954, p. 26.

68. *Ibid.,* p. 27.

69. Standing Committee on Banking and Commerce, *Minutes of Proceedings and Evidence,* 1956, p. 374.

70. *Ibid.,* p. 375.

71. Standing Committee on Banking and Commerce, *Proceedings . . . Decennial Revision of the Bank Act,* 1954, p. 492.

72. *Debates,* 1956, p. 7352.

73. *Ibid.,* p. 7459.

74. *Ibid.,* pp. 945–948.

75. *Debates,* 1957, pp. 2768–72.

76. *Ibid.,* pp. 3004–07.

77. *Ibid.,* pp. 2817–42.

78. See, for example, *Debates,* 1956, p. 1334.

79. *Debates,* 1956, p. 2127.

80. *Debates,* 1957, p. 3005.

81. *Debates,* 1945, 2d sess., p. 2015. See also pp. 2000 and 2063.

82. See, for example, Standing Committee on Public Accounts, *Minutes of Proceedings and Evidence,* 1951, p. 124; 1945, p. 1890; 1939, p. 186, respectively.

Chapter 4

THE PILOTS

1. *Debates,* 1952–53, p. 3423.

2. *Ibid.*

3. *Debates,* 1936, pp. 1262, 1412.

4. *Ibid.,* p. 1262.

5. *Ibid.,* p. 1412.

6. *Debates,* 1955, pp. 1510–13.

7. *Ibid.,* p. 1517.

8. *Debates,* 1956, pp. 7407–08.

9. President of Park Steamship Company Limited; director of Crown Assets Disposal Corporation and of Export Credits Insurance Corporation; member of the Northwest Territories Council and of the Court Martial Appeal Board.

10. Revised Statutes of Canada (1952), c. 242, s. 7.

11. The third member is a member of the Canadian Maritime Commission, but this is now a minor responsibility, as was noted above.

12. Quoted in J. E. Hodgetts, "Administration and Politics: The Case of the Canadian Broadcasting Corporation," *Canadian Journal of Economics and Political Science,* XII (November 1946), 454–469, at 455, note 4.

13. "The Public Corporation in Canada," *Public Administration,* XXVIII (Winter 1950), 283–294, at 288–289, quoted by permission of the Hon. Editor, D. N. Chester.

14. *Revised Statutes of Canada* (1952), c. 42, s. 3.

15. Standing Committee on Banking and Commerce, *Minutes of Proceedings and Evidence,* 1956, p. 348.

16. Joint Committee of the Senate and the House of Commons on the Federal District Commission, *Minutes of Proceedings and Evidence,* 1956, pp. 17–18.

17. Both of these arrangements have been included in the organic statutes of the Bank of Canada, the Industrial Development Bank, the Central Mortgage and Housing Corporation, the National Research Council, and Trans-Canada Air Lines. See *Revised Statutes of Canada* (1952), c. 13, s. 13; c. 151, s. 7; c. 46, ss. 10, 12; c. 239, ss. 5, 11; c. 268, s. 5, respectively.

18. Sessional Committee on Railways and Shipping Owned, Operated and Controlled by the Government, *Minutes of Proceedings and Evidence,* 1950, p. 230. See also the hearings before the same committee in 1956, p. 296.

19. Special Committee on Broadcasting, *Minutes of Proceedings and Evidence,* 1952–53, p. 87. Judging from the 1955–56 annual report of the C.B.C., p. 59, each meeting lasted only about two or three days, on the average. The C.B.C. had an executive committee, as does the new corporation. The latter does not have a chairman of the board, however.

20. *Debates,* 1952–53, p. 3545.

21. *Debates,* 1955, p. 4825.

22. *Debates,* 1952–53, pp. 3545–46.

23. *Statutes of Canada,* 1–2 Eliz. II, c. 50 (1952–53).

24. Sessional Committee on Railways and Shipping, *Minutes of Proceedings and Evidence*, 1951, p. 236.

25. *Debates*, 1955, p. 6483; 1946, p. 4327; and 1952–53, p. 5424, respectively. In the last-named case, questioners were satisfied with the explanation that the corporation did not market farm products.

26. *Revised Statutes of Canada* (1952), c. 112, s. 3.

27. *Revised Statutes of Canada* (1952), c. 32, s. 3.

28. Special Committee on Broadcasting, *Minutes of Proceedings and Evidence*, 1952–53, p. 87.

29. *Ibid.*, p. 86.

30. *Revised Statutes of Canada* (1952), c. 273, s. 4. E. C. Desormeaux, secretary of the commission, has pointed out that this clause does not affect the government's right to consult "only one or all employers' and employees' organizations." Letter to the writer, Ottawa, Jan. 22, 1958.

31. *Revised Statutes of Canada* (1952), c. 13, s. 10. There can be no representatives from chartered banks, and if any director holds shares in a chartered bank he must dispose of them.

32. See the section on appointment and dismissal in Chapter 3, above.

33. *Revised Statutes of Canada*, c. 46, s. 6.

34. See Special Committee on Broadcasting, *Minutes of Proceedings and Evidence*, 1952–53, p. 88.

35. *Debates*, 1955, p. 3193.

36. *Debates*, 1952, p. 3635.

37. Taylor Cole, *Canadian Bureaucracy* (Durham, N.C., 1949), pp. 166–167.

38. *Revised Statutes of Canada* (1952), c. 32, s. 3.

39. See Special Committee on Broadcasting, *Minutes of Proceedings and Evidence*, 1952–53, p. 88.

40. *Revised Statutes of Canada* (1952), c. 13, s. 10; c. 46, s. 9.

41. *Debates*, 1957, pp. 3363, 3473.

42. *Ibid.*, p. 3401.

43. *Debates*, 1956, pp. 6114–15.

44. Agricultural Stabilization Board, Canadian Broadcasting Corporation, Canadian Maritime Commission, Canadian Wheat Board, Dominion Coal Board, Export Credits Insurance Corporation, and Fisheries Prices Support Board.

45. A maximum of fifteen members may be appointed to the "advisory council" of the Export Credits Insurance Corporation, while the Canadian Wheat Board's "advisory committee" may have no more than eleven members. *Revised Statutes of Canada* (1952), c. 105, s. 9 and c. 44, s. 9 respectively.

46. *Statutes of Canada*, 6 Eliz. II, c. 22, s. 5 (1957–58). After its

introduction, the bill was amended on suggestion of the Minister of Agriculture after representatives of the Canadian Federation of Agriculture and farm unions had expressed doubt as to whether the original language was sufficiently strong to guarantee that only farmers and their representatives would compose the committee. See *Debates,* 1957–58, pp. 2652–53.

47. *Statutes of Canada,* 25–26 Geo. V, c. 16, s. 11 (1935).
48. *Revised Statutes of Canada* (1952), c. 309, s. 7.
49. *Statutes of Canada,* 4–5 Eliz. II, c. 17 (1956).
50. *Revised Statutes of Canada* (1952), c. 32, s. 12.
51. Still other public affairs programs are prepared by the C.B.C. only after consultation with various private groups.
52. See the Board's *Annual Report* for 1955–56, p. 7.
53. *Debates,* 1957–58, p. 3823.
54. *Debates,* 1944, p. 1045.
55. Canadian Wheat Board, *Annual Report* (1954–55), p. 27.
56. Letter to the writer from A. W. Thomas, assistant general manager, Export Credits Insurance Corporation, Ottawa, Canada, June 11, 1958.
57. Federal District Commission, *Annual Report* (1955), p. 14.
58. *Ibid.*
59. In 1916 the government established the Honorary Advisory Council for Scientific and Industrial Research as an advisory body of eleven men responsible to a committee of six cabinet ministers. It still bears this name, although it was given corporate form and operational duties at a later date.
60. National Research Council, *Review* (1957), Ottawa, 1957, p. 13.
61. *Ibid.,* p. 12.
62. Atomic Energy of Canada Limited, *Annual Report* (1954–55), p. 5. Nevertheless, expressions of opinion from the committee as a whole or its individual members are borne in mind by the corporation in formulating its policies and programs, according to a letter from the corporation's secretary to the writer.
63. Letter to the writer from H. C. L. Ransom, executive director, Fisheries Prices Support Board, Ottawa, Feb. 21, 1958.
64. See the discussion of the board in the first section of this chapter and *Debates,* 1955, pp. 1509–17.
65. *Debates,* 1944, p. 5577.
66. *Ibid.* In view of the emphasis in the above quotation on not paying advisory committee members, it is interesting to note that members of the committee under the new Agricultural Stabilization Board apparently will be paid. See *Debates,* 1957–58, p. 2671.
67. H. L. Trueman, "Advisory Committees in Agriculture," paper

executorship of the estate of a large shareholder in a company that did a good deal of business with his department than was spent on corporations.

20. *Statutes of Canada,* 15–16 Geo. VI, c. 6 (1951, 2d sess.).

21. The number and title of the item, together with the inclusive pages of the *Debates,* 1956, in which the C.N.R. was discussed, are as follows. (1) "435. Departmental Administration, $1,777,100" (pp. 7021–44). (2) "Board of transport commissioners for Canada — 494. Administration, operation and maintenance, $867,930" (pp. 7400–05). (3) "497. Advances to national harbours board . . ." (p. 7417). A fourth item, dealing with a subsidy to the railroad to construct a branch line curiously produced no discussion of the C.N.R.

22. (1) "435. Departmental administration, $1,777,100" (pp. 2215–16, 4928). (2) "474. Air services administration, $816,760" (pp. 7377–90, 7392–95). (3) "Air transport board — 493. Salaries and other expenses . . ." (pp. 7399–7400).

23. Among the matters mentioned in 1956 were the following: the financial difficulties of the C.N.R., its need for increased financial independence, and its employees' grievances; financial status of the air lines vis-à-vis the C.N.R. and Mr. Howe's supervision of T.C.A. See *Debates,* 1956, pp. 4901–06, 4964–70. Properly speaking, debates under statutes making loans to corporations, as this one does, should be classified separately from debates on the estimates.

24. *Debates,* 1953–54, pp. 585–586.

25. *Debates,* 1951, 2d sess., p. 1371.

26. Acton Society Trust, *Accountability to Parliament* (Claygate, 1950), p. 17.

27. See, for example, *Debates,* 1956, pp. 2119–20 and 3563.

28. *Ibid.,* p. 6599.

29. *Ibid.,* pp. 5520–24, 6595–6603, 7024.

30. See, for example, *ibid.,* pp. 3515, 6221.

31. See, for example, *ibid.,* pp. 2119, 3752.

32. A. E. Buck, *Financing Canadian Government* (Chicago, 1949), p. 147. See also Harold G. Villard and W. W. Willoughby, *The Canadian Budgetary System* (New York, 1918), pp. 164–175.

33. Standing Committee on Public Accounts, *Minutes of Proceedings and Evidence,* 1956, p. 56. It should be noted that the *Canadian Government Publications Catalogue* (1953 Consolidated Edition) indicates that *Minutes of Proceedings and Evidence* are available for several more sessions of Parliament than the chairman indicated.

34. H. R. Balls, "Budgetary and Fiscal Accounting in the Government of Canada [Part II]," *Canadian Tax Journal,* IV (March-April 1956), 132–139, at 136.

35. Standing Committee on Public Accounts, *Minutes of Proceedings and Evidence*, 1951, 2d sess., opposite p. 111.

36. Those corporations having "outside" auditors are the Canadian National Railways, Canadian National (West Indies) Steamships Limited, Trans-Canada Air Lines, Central Mortgage and Housing Corporation, Bank of Canada, Industrial Development Bank, and Canadian Wheat Board. For the background, see Balls, "Financial Control," *Public Administration*, XXXI, 141.

37. Standing Committee on Public Accounts, *Minutes of Proceedings and Evidence*, 1956, p. 98.

38. *Ibid.*, p. 138.

39. Standing Committee on Public Accounts, *Minutes of Proceedings and Evidence*, 1951, 2d sess., pp. 137–138. See also *Debates*, 1951, 2d sess., p. 2006.

40. Standing Committee on Public Accounts, *Minutes of Proceedings and Evidence*, 1950, pp. 65 and 61, respectively.

41. Referring to a proposal to strengthen the British Public Accounts Committee, Herbert Morrison stated in 1950: "The chief difficulty about suggestions of this kind is that they re-introduce meticulous Parliamentary supervision by another route." "Public Control of the Socialized Industries," *Public Administration*, XXVIII (Spring 1950), 3–9, at 8. For an account of the presentation of rather similar views by heads of two nationalized industries, see Gweneth Gutch, "Nationalized Industries and the Public Accounts Committee, 1951–52," *Public Administration*, XXXI (Autumn 1953), 255–263.

42. Standing Committee on Public Accounts, *Minutes of Proceedings and Evidence*, 1950, pp. 61–63.

43. The National Research Council came before these committees only in 1956. A Special Committee on the National Research Council was set up for the 1956 session of Parliament.

44. During its 1956 meetings, the Sessional Committee on Railways and Shipping spent almost nineteen hours in questioning the presidents of the Canadian National Railways and Trans-Canada Air Lines on items in the corporations' annual reports, auditors' reports and budgets. Fleeting attention was also given to Canadian National (West Indies) Steamships Limited.

45. Sessional Committee on Railways and Shipping, *Minutes of Proceedings and Evidence*, 1956, pp. 92–101.

46. *Ibid.*, pp. 98–101.

47. *Ibid.*, pp. 198–203.

48. *Ibid.*, pp. 101–102.

49. *Ibid.*, pp. 295–296.

50. Standing Committee on Public Accounts, *Minutes of Proceedings and Evidence*, 1950, p. 67.

51. J. E. Hodgetts, "The Public Corporation in Canada," *Public Administration*, XXVIII (Winter 1950), 283–294, at 292. See also, by the same author, "Administration and Politics: The Case of the Canadian Broadcasting Corporation," *Canadian Journal of Economics and Political Science*, XII (November 1946), 454–469. It may be noted, in passing, that royal commissions have also "eased the political pressure" on the C.B.C. and that the latest Royal Commission on Broadcasting urged the C.B.C. to adopt a much more vigorous policy of public relations in order to counter the "devious propaganda" of the Canadian Association of Radio and Television Broadcasters. *Report* (Ottawa, 1957), pp. 137–139.

52. See Standing Committee on Public Accounts, *Minutes of Proceedings and Evidence*, 1950, pp. 64–65.

53. *Debates*, 1942, pp. 972–973; *Debates*, 1951, pp. 2004–06.

54. See Sessional Committee on Railways and Shipping, *Minutes of Proceedings and Evidence*, 1956, pp. 96 and 99.

55. See terms of the resolution appointing the committee on March 10, 1955. *Debates*, 1955, p. 1890.

56. Special Committee on Broadcasting, *Minutes of Proceedings and Evidence*, 1955, pp. 808–812.

Chapter 6

PUBLIC OWNERSHIP AND ACCOUNTABILITY

1. John Thurston, *Government Proprietary Corporations in the English-Speaking Countries* (Cambridge, Mass., 1937), pp. 98–99.

2. D. N. Chester, "Public Corporations and the Classification of Administrative Bodies," *Political Studies*, I (February 1953), 34–52, at 46.

3. The Agricultural Prices Support Board (now Agricultural Stabilization Board), Atomic Energy Control Board, Fisheries Prices Support Board, and National Research Council. See H. R. Balls, "Personnel Policy and Practices in Canadian Crown Corporations," Seminar Paper No. 97 (mimeo.), Seminar on Organization and Administration of Public Enterprises in the Industrial Field, Rangoon, March 1954.

4. See, for example, Deutsch, "Parliament and the Civil Service," *Queen's Quarterly*, XLIII, 571, and the statement of the present Prime Minister in 1950 that "we lack technical assistance for the examination of the [public]accounts." Standing Committee on Public Accounts, *Minutes of Proceedings and Evidence*, 1950, p. 57.

5. For a brief review, see Dawson, *The Government of Canada*, pp. 344–345.

6. Compare Ernest Davies, "Ministerial Control and Parliamentary Responsibility of Nationalized Industries," *Problems of Nationalized Industry*, ed. W. A. Robson (London, 1952), pp. 109–119, at 114–115.

7. Frank Milligan, "Financing the Canadian Crown Corporations: Capital Financing," Seminar Paper No. 68, (mimeo.), Seminar on Organization and Administration of Public Enterprises in the Industrial Field, Rangoon, March 1954, p. 4.

8. *Ibid.*, p. 2.

9. Both quotations are from *Debates*, 1946, p. 2482.

10. J. W. Grove, "British Public Corporations: Some Recent Developments," *Journal of Politics*, XVIII (November 1956), 651–677, at 671–672.

11. "Mr. Morrison's Views on Public Accountability," *Public Administration*, XXVIII (Autumn 1950), 176–178, at 176. The quotation actually was in reference to the boards of the nationalized industries. One commentator has made the interesting point that "two mutually exclusive types of relationships" are suggested in the British nationalization statutes: (1) "a scheme of limited control" in which a minister may give specific directions to a corporation, but the latter retains "residual authority"; and (2) a scheme "in which full control over the corporation's affairs runs in a direct line-of-command relationship from the board through the minister and ultimately to Parliament," and typified by the power to appoint and dismiss as well as the power to issue general directions. Lucile Sheppard Keyes, "Some Controversial Aspects of the Public Corporation," *Political Science Quarterly*, LXX (March 1955), 28–56, at 34–35.

12. *Debates*, 1955, p. 956.

13. *Ibid.*, p. 957.

Index